STUDY GUIDE

Superpower Relations and the Cold War, 1941-91

Edexcel - GCSE

app available

www.GCSEHistory.com

Published by Clever Lili Limited.

contact@cleverlili.com

First published 2020

ISBN 978-1-913887-04-9

Copyright notice

All rights reserved. No part of this publication may be reproduced in any form or by any means (including photocopying or storing it in any medium by electronic means and whether or not transiently or incidentally to some other use of this publication) with the written permission of the copyright owner. Applications for the copyright owner's written permission should be addressed to the publisher.

Clever Lili has made every effort to contact copyright holders for permission for the use of copyright material. We will be happy, upon notification, to rectify any errors or omissions and include any appropriate rectifications in future editions.

Cover by: Onur on Adobe Stock

Icons by: flaticon and freepik

Contributors: Lynn Harkin, Petia Hak

Edited by Paul Connolly and Rebecca Parsley

Design by Evgeni Veskov and Will Fox

All rights reserved

DISCOVER MORE OF OUR GCSE HISTORY STUDY GUIDES
GCSEHistory.com and Clever Lili

   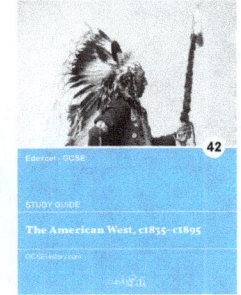

THE GUIDES ARE EVEN BETTER WITH OUR GCSE/IGCSE HISTORY WEBSITE APP AND MOBILE APP

GCSE History is a text and voice web and mobile app that allows you to easily revise for your GCSE/IGCSE exams wherever you are - it's like having your own personal GCSE history tutor. Whether you're at home or on the bus, GCSE History provides you with thousands of convenient bite-sized facts to help you pass your exams with flying colours. We cover all topics - with more than 120,000 questions - across the Edexcel, AQA and CIE exam boards.

Contents

How to use this book 6
What is this book about? 7
Revision suggestions 9

Timelines
Superpower Relations and the Cold War, 1941-91 13

The Origins of the Cold War
Cold War 16
Grand Alliance 17
Tehran Conference, 1943 18
Yalta Conference, Feb 1945 19
Potsdam Conference, July 1945 21
The Long Telegram, 1946 22
The Novikov Telegram, 1946 23

Creation of the Satellite States
Satellite States, 1946-49 23
Poland 24
Czechoslovakia 25
Hungary 26
Bulgaria 27
Romania 27
Yugoslavia 28

The Cold War Begins
Iron Curtain Speech, 1946 29
Truman Doctrine, 1947 30
Marshall Plan, 1947 31
Cominform, 1947 32
Comecon, 1949 33

The Berlin Crisis, 1948
Berlin Blockade, 1948-49 34
Berlin Airlift, 1948-49 35

The Military Response
NATO, 1949 36
Warsaw Pact, 1955 37
Arms Race 37

The Hungarian Uprising, 1956
De-Stalinisation 39
Hungarian Uprising, 1956 40

The Berlin Crisis, 1958 to 1961
Berlin Crisis, 1958-61 42
The Berlin Wall, 1961-62 43

The Cuban Crisis, 1959 to 1962
Cuban Revolution, 1959 44
Bay of Pigs, 1961 45
Cuban Missile Crisis, October 1962 46
Hotline, 1963 48
Limited Test Ban Treaty, 1963 49
Outer Space Treaty, 1967 49
Nuclear Non-Proliferation Treaty, 1968 50

The Czechoslovakian Crisis, 1968
Prague Spring, 1968 51
Brezhnev Doctrine, 1968 53

The Détente Period
Détente 54
SALT 1, 1972 55
Helsinki Accords, 1975 57
Apollo-Soyuz Mission, 1975 58
SALT 2, 1979 58

The Collapse of Détente
Soviet Invasion of Afghanistan, 1979 59
Carter Doctrine, 1980 60
President Ronald Reagan, 1981 61
Strategic Defense Initiative (SDI), 1983 62

Gorbachev's New Thinking
Mikhail Gorbachev, 1985-1991 63
Perestroika 64
Glasnost 64

The Impact of Reagan and Gorbachev
Reagan and Gorbachev's Relationship 65
Geneva Summit, 1985 65
Reykjavik Summit, 1986 66
Washington Summit, 1987 67
Intermediate-Range Nuclear Force (INF) Treaty, 1987 67
Moscow Summit, 1988 68

Gorbachev and Bush
Malta Summit, 1988 69
Treaty on Conventional Armed Forces in Europe, 1990 69
Strategic Arms Reduction Treaty (START I) 1991 70

The Collapse of the USSR
The Collapse of Soviet Control of Eastern Europe, 1989-1990 .. 70
Fall of the Berlin Wall, 1989 71

Gorbachev's Fall from Power 72
The Collapse of the USSR, 1990-91 73

People of the Cold War

Hafizullah Amin 74
Prime Minister Attlee 74
Fulgencio Batista 74
Leonid Brezhnev 75
President Jimmy Carter 75
Prime Minister Churchill 76
Alexander Dubček 76
President Eisenhower 77
Mikhail Gorbachev 78
George Kennan 79
President John F Kennedy 80
Nikita Khrushchev 81
George Marshall 82
Imre Nagy 82
Nikolai Novikov 83
Antonin Novotný 83
President Roosevelt 83
Nur Muhammad Taraki 84
President Harry Truman 84

Glossary 86
Index 89

HOW TO USE THIS BOOK

In this study guide, you will see a series of icons, highlighted words and page references. The key below will help you quickly establish what these mean and where to go for more information.

Icons

 WHAT questions cover the key events and themes.

 WHO questions cover the key people involved.

 WHEN questions cover the timings of key events.

 WHERE questions cover the locations of key moments.

 WHY questions cover the reasons behind key events.

 HOW questions take a closer look at the way in which events, situations and trends occur.

 IMPORTANCE questions take a closer look at the significance of events, situations, and recurrent trends and themes.

 DECISIONS questions take a closer look at choices made at events and situations during this era.

Highlighted words

Abdicate - occasionally, you will see certain words highlighted within an answer. This means that, if you need it, you'll find an explanation of the word or phrase in the glossary which starts on **page 86**.

Page references

Tudor *(p.7)* - occasionally, a certain subject within an answer is covered in more depth on a different page. If you'd like to learn more about it, you can go directly to the page indicated.

WHAT IS THIS BOOK ABOUT?

Superpower relations and the Cold War, 1941-91 is the period study that investigates the causes of the Cold War, three of its key crises and the reasons it ended. You will study the role key individuals played during the Cold War, as well as how it impacted specific countries. You will focus on crucial events during this period, and study the political, economic and military changes that occurred.

Purpose
This study will enable you to understand the complexities of the Cold War. You will investigate themes such as communism, capitalism, sphere of influence, satellite states, containment and the arms race. This course will help you develop the historical skills of explanation and analysis of key events to demonstrate your understanding of how they are connected.

Topics
Superpower relations and the Cold War, 1941-91, is divided into 3 key topics:
- Topic 1 looks at the origins of the Cold War and the reasons for increasing tension between 1943 and 1956. You will investigate how and why the divisions between the superpowers grew, politically, economically and militarily.
- Topic 2 looks at the three key Cold War crises between 1958 and 1970. You will investigate the causes, main events and consequences of the Berlin crisis (1958-61), the Cuban Missile Crisis, and the Prague Spring.
- Topic 3 looks at the end of the Cold War between 1970 and 1991. You will study how far tension was eased during the period of détente and the reasons why it ended with the USSR's invasion of Afghanistan. You will investigate the roles of President Reagan and Premier Gorbachev in bringing the Cold War to an end. The topic culminates with the collapse of the USSR.

Key Individuals
Some of the key individuals studied on this course include:
- President Roosevelt.
- Prime Minister Churchill.
- Premier Stalin.
- President Truman.
- Premier Khrushchev.
- Premier Brezhnev.
- Fidel Castro.
- President John F Kennedy.
- President Ronald Reagan.
- Premier Mikhail Gorbachev.

Key Events
Some of the key events you will study on this course include:
- The three wartime conferences.
- The Berlin Blockade and Airlift.
- The Arms Race.
- The Cuban Missile Crisis.
- Détente.
- The Soviet invasion of Afghanistan.
- The Fall of the Berlin Wall.

Assessment
Superpower relations and the Cold War, 1941-91, forms part of paper 2 which you have a total of 1 hour 45 minutes to complete. You should spend approximately 50 minutes on this section, booklet P, of the paper. There will be 3 exam questions which will assess what you have learnt on the Superpower relations and the Cold War, 1941-91. For Question 3, you will have to select two from three options.
- Question 1 is worth 8 marks. This question will require you to identify two consequences of an event. You will need to support the identified consequences with facts and explain how they occurred.

WHAT IS THIS BOOK ABOUT?

- Question 2 is worth 8 marks. This question will require you to write an analytical narrative account of an event or time period. You will need to describe what happened as well as explain how and why events are connected.
- Question 3 is worth 8 marks. This question will require you to explain the importance of two events, people or developments in relation to specific situations. You will need to explain what difference the event made to the specific situation.

REVISION SUGGESTIONS

Revision! A dreaded word. Everyone knows it's coming, everyone knows how much it helps with your exam performance, and everyone struggles to get started! We know you want to do the best you can in your GCSEs, but schools aren't always clear on the best way to revise. This can leave students wondering:

- ✓ How should I plan my revision time?
- ✓ How can I beat procrastination?
- ✓ What methods should I use? Flash cards? Re-reading my notes? Highlighting?

Luckily, you no longer need to guess at the answers. Education researchers have looked at all the available revision studies, and the jury is in. They've come up with some key pointers on the best ways to revise, as well as some thoughts on popular revision methods that aren't so helpful. The next few pages will help you understand what we know about the best revision methods.

How can I beat procrastination?

This is an age-old question, and it applies to adults as well! Have a look at our top three tips below.

⊚ Reward yourself

When we think a task we have to do is going to be boring, hard or uncomfortable, we often put if off and do something more 'fun' instead. But we often don't really enjoy the 'fun' activity because we feel guilty about avoiding what we should be doing. Instead, get your work done and promise yourself a reward after you complete it. Whatever treat you choose will seem all the sweeter, and you'll feel proud for doing something you found difficult. Just do it!

⊚ Just do it!

We tend to procrastinate when we think the task we have to do is going to be difficult or dull. The funny thing is, the most uncomfortable part is usually making ourselves sit down and start it in the first place. Once you begin, it's usually not nearly as bad as you anticipated.

⊚ Pomodoro technique

The pomodoro technique helps you trick your brain by telling it you only have to focus for a short time. Set a timer for 20 minutes and focus that whole period on your revision. Turn off your phone, clear your desk, and work. At the end of the 20 minutes, you get to take a break for five. Then, do another 20 minutes. You'll usually find your rhythm and it becomes easier to carry on because it's only for a short, defined chunk of time.

Spaced practice

We tend to arrange our revision into big blocks. For example, you might tell yourself: "This week I'll do all my revision for the Cold War, then next week I'll do the Medicine Through Time unit."

REVISION SUGGESTIONS

This is called **massed practice**, because all revision for a single topic is done as one big mass.

But there's a better way! Try **spaced practice** instead. Instead of putting all revision sessions for one topic into a single block, space them out. See the example below for how it works.

This means planning ahead, rather than leaving revision to the last minute - but the evidence strongly suggests it's worth it. You'll remember much more from your revision if you use **spaced practice** rather than organising it into big blocks. Whichever method you choose, though, remember to reward yourself with breaks.

Spaced practice (more effective):

week 1	week 2	week 3	week 4
Topic 1	Topic 1	Topic 1	Topic 1
Topic 2	Topic 2	Topic 2	Topic 2
Topic 3	Topic 3	Topic 3	Topic 3
Topic 4	Topic 4	Topic 4	Topic 4

Massed practice (less effective)

week 1	week 2	week 3	week 4
Topic 1	Topic 2	Topic 3	Topic 4

REVISION SUGGESTIONS

 What methods should I use to revise?

        Self-testing/flash cards   *Self explanation/mind-mapping*

 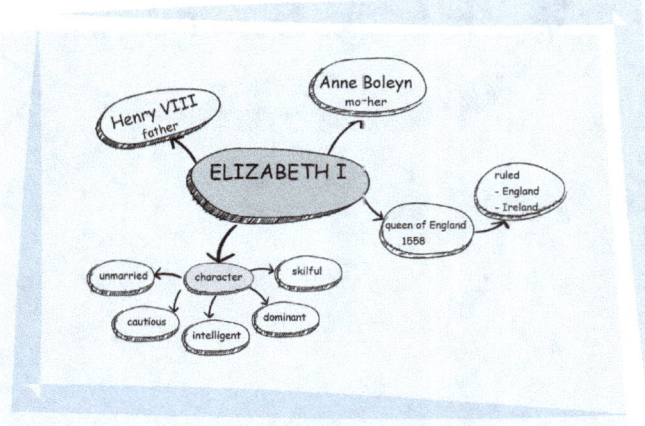

The research shows a clear winner for revision methods - **self-testing**. A good way to do this is with **flash cards.** Flash cards are really useful for helping you recall short – but important – pieces of information, like names and dates.

Side A - question   Side B - answer

Write questions on one side of the cards, and the answers on the back. This makes answering the questions and then testing yourself easy. Put all the cards you get right in a pile to one side, and only repeat the test with the ones you got wrong - this will force you to work on your weaker areas.

pile with right answers   pile with wrong answers

As this book has a quiz question structure itself, you can use it for this technique.

Another good revision method is **self-explanation**. This is where you explain how and why one piece of information from your course linked with another piece.

This can be done with **mind-maps**, where you draw the links and then write explanations for how they connect. For example, President Truman is connected with anti-communism because of the Truman Doctrine.

REVISION SUGGESTIONS

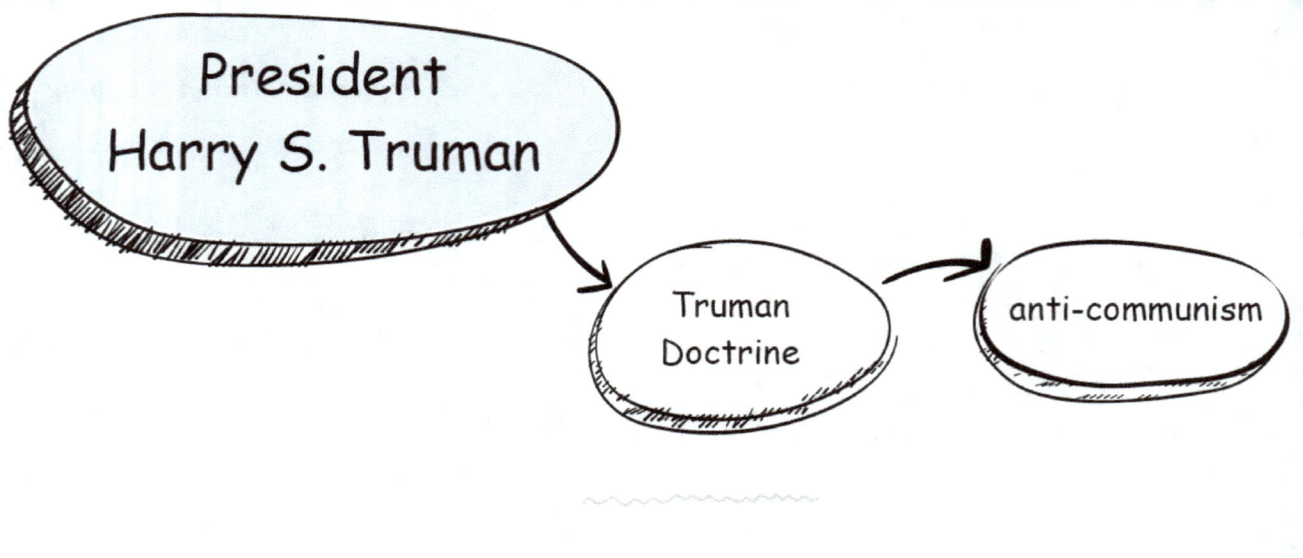

Review	Self-Test	Apply
Start by highlighting or re-reading to create your flashcards for self-testing.	Test yourself with flash cards. Make mind maps to explain the concepts.	Apply your knowledge on practice exam questions.

Which revision techniques should I be cautious about?

Highlighting and **re-reading** are not necessarily bad strategies - but the research does say they're less effective than flash cards and mind-maps.

Highlighting		Re-reading

If you do use these methods, make sure they are **the first step to creating flash cards**. Really engage with the material as you go, rather than switching to autopilot.

SUPERPOWER RELATIONS AND THE COLD WAR, 1941-91

TIMELINE

- **1941** — Grand Alliance formed (p.17)
- **1943** — *November 1945* - Tehran Conference (p.18)
- **1945**
  - *February 1945* - Yalta Conference (p.19)
  - *July 1945* - Potsdam Conference (p.21)
- **1946**
  - *February 1946* - Long Telegram (p.22)
  - *September 1946* - Novikov Telegram (p.23)
  - *March 1946* - Iron Curtain' speech (p.29)
- **1947**
  - *March 1947* - Truman Doctrine (p.30)
  - *September 1947* - Cominform created (p.31)
- **1948**
  - Marshall Plan (p.32)
  - *June 1948* - Berlin Blockade began (p.34)
- **1949**
  - USSR atomic bomb test (p.38)
  - *May 1949* - Berlin Airlift ended (p.35)
  - *January 1949* - Comecon created (p.33)
  - *April 1949* - NATO created (p.36)
- **1955** — *May 1955* - Warsaw Pact created (p.37)
- **1956** — *July 1956* - Hungarian Uprising began (p.40)
- **1959** — Geneva Summit (p.42)
- **1961**
  - *April 1961* - Bay of Pigs (p.45)
  - *August 1961* - Berlin Wall built (p.43)
- **1962** — *October 1962* - Cuban Missile Crisis (p.46)
- **1963** — *August 1963* - Limited Test Ban Treaty (p.49)
- **1968**
  - *January 1968* - Prague Spring began (p.51)
  - *September 1968* - Brezhnev Doctrine (p.53)
- **1972** — *May 1972* - SALT I (p.55)

SUPERPOWER RELATIONS AND THE COLD WAR, 1941-91

COLD WAR

Although the shooting war is over, we are in the midst of a cold war which is getting warmer.' - Bernard Baruch, 1947

What was the Cold War?
The Cold War was a state of hostility that existed between the USSR and the USA in the second half of the 20th century.

What is the definition of a cold war?
A cold war is a conflict in which there is no direct fighting between the two sides. It is fought through economic and political actions.

When was the Cold War?
The Cold War lasted from 1945 to 1991.

Who was involved in the Cold War?
The Cold War was between the USA and its allies, and the Soviet Union, its satellite states and its allies.

What were the long-term causes of the Cold War?
There are 7 main reasons the Cold War happened:
- In October 1917, the Bolsheviks seized power in Russia. By 1921 they had created the first communist state. They were anti-capitalism and wanted to spread the communist revolution across the world.
- America and Britain did not trust the USSR as Russia had withdrawn from the First World War in 1917, despite being a member of the Triple Entente with Britain and France.
- The USSR did not trust the USA, France and Britain because they sent troops to fight against the Bolsheviks in the Russian Civil War.
- In the 1920s, the USA suffered from the First Red Scare and was hostile towards the USSR.
- The USSR was angry it was not recognised as a country by the USA until 1933.
- The relationship between the USSR and the West deteriorated before the Second World War. The Soviet Union was angry at not being invited to the Munich Conference in 1938.
- When the USSR signed the Nazi-Soviet Pact in 1939, Britain and France were horrified.

How was the Cold War fought?
The Cold War was fought in 7 key ways:
- Propaganda.
- Spying or espionage, such as using spy planes to take photographs.
- An arms race to have the most developed weapons, particularly nuclear missiles.
- A space race competing for success in space, such as being the first nation to put a man on the moon.
- Financial aid or loans to other countries to gain their support.
- Proxy wars, where the USA and the USSR became involved in conflicts in other countries. An example is the Korean War of 1950-53.
- Threats made by either side.

What created tension between the Soviet Union and the USA at the beginning of the Cold War?
The ideological differences between the superpowers created tension between them. The Soviet Union supported communism, whereas the USA and Britain were capitalist countries.

What were the different ideologies in the Cold War?
The Cold War was a result of ideological differences between the two sides:
- The USSR was communist. Communism is a system where there is no private ownership of land, property or business. The aim is to achieve economic equality for the benefit of the people through central control of the state economy.
- The USA was capitalist. Capitalism is a system where individuals are free to own land, property and businesses to create wealth and accept there will be economic inequality as a result.

Why were the USA and the USSR considered superpowers during the Cold War?
The USSR and the USA were considered to be superpowers because they possessed 3 key things:
- Massive military might, including nuclear weapons.
- Economic might.
- The ability to dominate other countries.

Why was Stalin distrustful of Truman at the beginning at the Cold War?
Joseph Stalin was distrustful of Harry S Truman for 3 key reasons:
- Truman was anti-communist.
- He tried to control the Potsdam meeting.
- He successfully tested the atomic bomb without consulting Stalin and used it in the Hiroshima and Nagasaki bombings in the days after Potsdam.

Why did Britain ally closely with the USA at the beginning at the Cold War?
Britain was concerned about communism spreading. The nation's economy was severely impacted after the Second World War so it couldn't act against the Soviet Union alone.

> **DID YOU KNOW?**
>
> **The first known mention of the term 'Cold War' was made by English author George Orwell.**
> He mentioned it in an essay entitled 'You and the Atomic Bomb', written in 1945.

GRAND ALLIANCE
'The Russian danger... is our danger.' - Winston Churchill

What was the Grand Alliance?
The Grand Alliance was a military and political coalition against the Axis powers of Nazi Germany, Italy, and Japan during the Second World War.

When was the Grand Alliance formed?
The Grand Alliance began after the USA entered the Second World War. The alliance was formally signed by the USA, the Soviet Union and Great Britain on New Year's Day, 1942, and lasted until 1945.

Who was part of the Grand Alliance?
The Grand Alliance consisted of the three major Allies of the Second World War - the Soviet Union, the United States, and Great Britain.

Why was the Grand Alliance formed?
The sole purpose of the Grand Alliance was to defeat the Axis powers - Nazi Germany, fascist Italy and Imperial Japan.

Why was there tension in the Grand Alliance?
Although they were fighting the Nazi threat together, there were 3 main reasons for tension between the countries of the Grand Alliance during the Second World War:

- Both sides kept secrets. Stalin refused to share battle plans with Britain and France; when German troops surrendered in Italy, Britain and the US did not include the USSR in the discussions.
- Stalin believed the USA had deliberately delayed opening a second front in France until 1944 so the USSR would be weakened fighting Nazi Germany on its own.
- The two sides had opposing ideologies and did not trust each other.

How did the Grand Alliance cooperate during the Second World War?
The public was presented with a positive image of the Grand Alliance, and the three countries did help each other in 3 key ways:

- British merchant ships helped take supplies to the USSR.
- America included the USSR in its Lend-Lease programme, which meant it lent and sold military equipment to help defeat Germany.
- The USSR lost 26 million people fighting the Nazis after 1941, but this meant Germany's army was tied down and allowed Britain and America to plan and launch D-Day.

DID YOU KNOW?

The Grand Alliance is often referred to as a 'marriage of convenience'.
The USSR and the USA put aside their ideological differences to fight a common enemy - Nazi Germany.

TEHRAN CONFERENCE, 1943
The Tehran Conference was held to decide how the Second World War would be won.

What was the Tehran Conference?
The Tehran Conference was the first of three strategic meetings between the USA, Britain and the Soviet Union to discuss Nazi Germany and how to end the war.

Who attended the Tehran Conference?
The three Allied leaders who attended the Tehran Conference were:

- President Franklin D Roosevelt of the United States.
- General Secretary Joseph Stalin of the USSR.

- Prime Minister Winston Churchill *(p.76)* of the United Kingdom.

Where was the Tehran Conference held?
It was held at the Soviet Union's embassy in Tehran, Iran.

When was the Tehran Conference held?
The Tehran Conference was held from November to December, 1943.

Why was the Tehran Conference important?
The Tehran Conference was important for 3 main reasons:
- It led to a better relationship between the USA, Britain and the USSR.
- They were working together to defeat Nazi Germany, fascist Italy and Imperial Japan.
- They also discussed plans for the UN and ending the war.

What decisions were taken at the Tehran Conference?
There were 5 important decisions made at the Tehran Conference:
- It was decided the USA and Britain would open a second front by invading Europe through Nazi-occupied France.
- The USSR would invade Nazi Germany from the east.
- The USSR would invade Japan once Nazi Germany was defeated.
- The Polish border would be moved to the west, so Poland would gain territory from Germany and lose it to the USSR from the east.
- An international organisation would be created to settle international disagreements once the war was over. This would eventually become the United Nations.

What signs of tension were there at the Tehran Conference?
There were 2 key signs of tension at the Tehran Conference:
- Churchill *(p.76)* wanted the second front to be opened up in the Balkans, not in France.
- Roosevelt viewed Britain's colonialism as a greater threat than communism.

> **DID YOU KNOW?**
> Tehran was the first time Roosevelt, Churchill and Stalin met.

YALTA CONFERENCE, FEB 1945
The Yalta Conference was held to decide what would happen after the war.

What was the Yalta Conference?
The Yalta Conference was the second of three strategic meetings between the USA, Britain and the Soviet Union to discuss winning the war and post-war Europe.

Where was the Yalta Conference held?
The Yalta Conference took place in Yalta in the USSR.

When was the Yalta Conference held?

The Yalta Conference was held in February 1945.

Who attended the Yalta Conference?

The three Allied leaders present at the Yalta Conference were:
- President Roosevelt of the USA.
- General Secretary Stalin of the USSR.
- Prime Minister Churchill *(p.76)* of Great Britain.

What decisions were taken at the Yalta Conference?

There were 11 important decisions made at the Yalta Conference.
- The superpowers agreed on the Declaration of Liberated Europe which guaranteed all countries freed from Nazi control the right to hold democratic and free elections.
- Nazi Germany and Berlin would be divided into four zones controlled by the USA, Britain, France and the Soviet Union.
- Germany would be reduced in size.
- Germany would be demilitarised.
- Germany would be ordered to pay reparations.
- Nazi war criminals would be tried after the war was over and the Nazi Party banned.
- Poland would fall under the Soviet sphere of influence.
- Poland would be run under a democratically elected government.
- Eastern Europe would have free elections.
- The USSR would declare war on Japan 3 months after Nazi Germany was defeated.
- The United Nations was created.

What disagreements were there at the Yalta Conference?

There were 3 main disagreements at the Yalta Conference:
- The USSR wanted Germany to pay high reparations; Britain and the USA disagreed.
- Britain and the USA wanted Germany to recover, whereas the USSR wanted to keep Germany weak.
- Stalin wanted the Polish-German border to be much further to the west and desired a 'friendly' Polish government. Britain and the USA were worried this would mean Poland would be controlled by the USSR.

DID YOU KNOW?

The Yalta Conference was the final summit attended by Stalin, Roosevelt and Churchill.

President Roosevelt died before the Potsdam Conference and Churchill lost the general election to the Labour Party in July 1945.

POTSDAM CONFERENCE, JULY 1945

There was significant tension between the USSR and the USA at the Potsdam Conference over the issue of the atomic bomb.

What was the Potsdam Conference?
The Potsdam Conference was the third and final meeting between the USA, Britain and the Soviet Union to discuss Nazi Germany and the future of Europe.

Where was the Potsdam Conference held?
The Potsdam Conference was held in Potsdam, Germany.

When was the Potsdam Conference held?
The Potsdam Conference took place between July and August 1945.

Who attended the Potsdam Conference?
The three Allied leaders who met at Potsdam were:
- President Harry Truman *(p.84)* of the United States.
- Prime Minister Clement Attlee of Great Britain.
- Premier Joseph Stalin of the Soviet Union.

Why did the leaders at the Potsdam Conference change?
Leadership of two Allied nations had changed since the Yalta Conference *(p.19)*. Roosevelt died in April 1945 and Churchill *(p.76)* lost the British general election in July.

What disagreements were there at the Potsdam Conference?
There were 4 key areas of disagreement:
- The USA and Britain were unhappy Stalin had removed the non-communists from the Polish Provisional Government of National Unity.
- The USA and Britain were unhappy Stalin had not allowed free elections in eastern Europe. Stalin was angry as he thought the West was interfering.
- Truman deliberately delayed the Potsdam meeting so America could test the atomic bomb. When Truman informed Stalin about the USA's successful test, Stalin was very angry not to have been told beforehand.
- Truman was very anti-communist and wanted to get 'tough' with Stalin.

What decisions were taken at the Potsdam Conference?
There were 8 important decisions made at the Potsdam Conference:
- The Nazi Party was banned.
- War criminals were to be prosecuted.
- Germany was to be reduced in size.
- Germany would be divided into four occupied zones controlled by the USA, Britain, France and the Soviet Union.
- Berlin would also be divided into four occupied zones controlled by the USA, Britain, France and the Soviet Union.
- All economic decisions about Germany must be agreed to by all four powers in the Allied Control Council.
- A Council of Foreign Ministers was set up to organise the rebuilding of Europe.
- It was decided the Soviet Union would receive 25% of the industrial output from the other three occupied zones.

DID YOU KNOW?

Roosevelt's death of a haemorrhagic stroke in 1945 before the Potsdam Conference was unexpected and shocked both America and the world.

Half a million people attended his funeral procession.

THE LONG TELEGRAM, 1946

'It is clear that the main element of any United States policy towards the Soviet Union must be that of a long-term, patient, but firm and vigilant, containment of Russian expansive tendencies.'

What was the 'Long Telegram'?
The Long Telegram was a secret report sent by the US Ambassador in the Soviet Union, George Kennan, to President Truman.

When was the 'Long Telegram' sent?
The 'Long Telegram' was sent on 22nd February, 1946.

Who sent the 'Long Telegram'?
George Kennan, the US Ambassador in the Soviet Union, sent the 'Long Telegram'.

Where was the 'Long Telegram' sent?
The 'Long Telegram' was sent to Washington from the United States Embassy in Moscow.

What did the 'Long Telegram' say?
The 'Long Telegram' stated:
- The USSR was a threat to capitalism and should be eliminated.
- The USSR was building its military power.
- Peace between the USA and the USSR was not possible.
- The USSR was determined to expand.

DID YOU KNOW?

The 'Long Telegram' got its name because it was so much longer than a normal telegram.

It was over 5000 words, whereas telegrams were usually very brief. This showed the urgency of Kennan's message.

THE NOVIKOV TELEGRAM, 1946

The Novikov Telegram was very influential on the USSR's behaviour in eastern Europe.

What was the Novikov Telegram?
The Novikov Telegram was a secret report sent to Stalin.

When was the Novikov Telegram sent?
It was sent in September 1946.

Who sent the Novikov Telegram?
Nikolai Novikov, the Soviet Ambassador in the USA, sent the Novikov Telegram.

Where was the Novikov Telegram sent?
The Novikov Telegram was sent from the Soviet Embassy in Washington to Moscow.

What did the Novikov Telegram contain?
The Novikov Telegram stated that:
- ✓ The USA wanted to be the world's leading power.
- ✓ The USSR was the only power that could stand up to them.
- ✓ The USA was preparing for war against the Soviets.

DID YOU KNOW?

Novikov wrote in his telegram: 'All of these facts show clearly that a decisive role in the realization of plans for world dominance by the United States is played by its armed forces.'

SATELLITE STATES, 1946-49

After the Second World War, Stalin insisted on a protective 'buffer' of satellite states for the USSR.

What were the Soviet satellite states?
The Soviet satellite states were countries in eastern Europe under the political, economic and military influence of the USSR.

Who were the Soviet satellite states?
They were Poland, Czechoslovakia, Hungary, Romania, Bulgaria and East Germany.

When were the Soviet satellite states created?
The satellite states were created between 1946 and 1949.

What methods were used to create the Soviet satellite states?
There are 2 key things to note about the methods used:

- In the late 1940s, Stalin installed communist leaders in eastern European countries using 'salami tactics'.
- The term 'salami tactics' was coined by the communist Hungarian leader, Matyas Rakosi, to describe how Stalin dealt with opposition 'slice by slice'.

 ### How were the Soviet satellite states created?

There were 5 main ways in which the Soviet Union took over eastern European countries:

- The Red Army supported communists and intimidated the opposition. They acted as an occupying force.
- Elections were held and as a result the communists were part of coalition governments.
- The communists worked in coalitions to undermine the government and held key positions, such as head of the police, so they could arrest and murder opponents.
- Propaganda was used to label any opposition party or leader a fascist to boost support for communist parties or to demonise democratic politicians.
- Once in government, communist parties, aided by the security forces, rigged elections to ensure they remained in power.

 ### What was the importance of the Soviet satellite states?

The satellite states helped the Soviet Union in 4 key ways:

- It meant the USSR had gained a large territory with which it could trade.
- They enhanced its power.
- In theory, they strengthened communism.
- They acted as a buffer zone to protect the USSR from invasion.

 ### What were the different points of view about the Soviet satellite states?

There are 2 key things to note about how satellite states are viewed:

- Stalin viewed the satellite states as a necessary buffer against future invasion from Germany in particular.
- However, Britain and the USA saw them as a threat to the West.

> **DID YOU KNOW?**
>
> The countries of eastern Europe were called satellite states in the west because they were effectively controlled by the USSR and were positioned close around its border, like satellites around a planet.

POLAND

'Fitting communism onto Poland is like putting a saddle on a cow.'
- Stalin, 1944

 ### What is Poland?

Poland is a country in central Europe.

 ### When did Poland become a satellite state?

Soviet control was established over Poland in 1947.

How did Poland become a satellite state?

Poland became a satellite state through 5 key events:

- Before the Second World War, Poland had a mostly agricultural economy and a traditional hatred of the USSR.
- During the Second World War, it was at first divided between Germany and the USSR, and then completely occupied by Germany.
- During the war, it had two governments - one based in London, and the other in the Polish town of Lublin.
- After it was liberated, Soviet troops remained and a new government was formed in June 1945 dominated by communist-sympathising 'Lublin' Poles.
- Opposition leaders were assassinated and imprisoned before a rigged vote in 1947 gave the communists 80% of the vote.

> **DID YOU KNOW?**
>
> In August 1941, the USSR released thousands of Poles who had been taken prisoner in 1939.
>
> They formed eight divisions of the 'Anders Army' and fought alongside British troops in the Middle East.

CZECHOSLOVAKIA

'Victorious February!'
The name given to the month in which Czechoslovakia became communist.

What was Czechoslovakia?

Czechoslovakia was a country in central Europe.

When did Czechoslovakia become a satellite state?

Czechoslovakia came under Soviet control in 1948.

How did Czechoslovakia become a satellite state?

Czechoslovakia became a satellite state through 5 key events:

- Czechoslovakia had a democracy and strong support for the communists before the war. It was invaded by Germany in 1939.
- After the war, Soviet troops left the country and elections put the communists in charge of a coalition government.
- The communists gradually took control of government ministries.
- Communists arrested political opponents and Jan Masaryk, a non-communist politician, was murdered in March 1948.
- All non-communist members of the government resigned in February 1948, and the communists assumed complete control.

> **DID YOU KNOW?**
>
> **In March 1948, during a communist purge of the Czechoslovakian government, the pro-American Jans Masaryk was found dead beneath his window.**
>
> Jan Masaryk expressed interest in Czechoslovakia receiving aid under the Marshall Plan. According to official reports he committed suicide by jumping from a window. A police report in 2004 ruled he was murdered.

HUNGARY

'Hungary conquered and in chains...' - Albert Camus

What is Hungary?
Hungary is a landlocked country in central Europe.

When did Hungary become a satellite state?
Soviet control was established over Hungary in 1948.

How did Hungary become a satellite state?
Hungary became a satellite state through 6 key events:

- Hungary had an agricultural-based economy and little support for the communists. It was a German ally in the Second World War.
- Soviet troops remained in the country after liberation.
- In November 1945, elections gave communists 17% of the vote, but they were put in control of the Ministry of the Interior.
- They used secret police to control and intimidate opposition politicians.
- In 1947 rigged elections gave the communists control of the coalition government.
- The Social Democratic Party and Communist Party merged in 1948, giving the communists control of Hungary.

> **DID YOU KNOW?**
>
> **The communist leader of Hungary was Matyas Rakosi.**
>
> He was known by Hungarians as 'the Bald Butcher'.

BULGARIA

'I feel deep anxiety because of...[the USSR's] overwhelming influence in the Balkans.' - Churchill to Truman, 1945

What is Bulgaria?

Bulgaria is a country in south-eastern Europe.

When did Bulgaria become a satellite state?

Bulgaria came under Soviet control in 1947.

How did Bulgaria become a satellite state?

Bulgaria became a satellite state through 5 key events:

- Before the Second World War, Bulgaria was a monarchy with strong links to Russia. However, during the war it was allied with Germany.
- Soviet troops remained there after the war.
- The communists joined the Fatherland Front, a coalition government with other parties. However, they then purged it of other political groups.
- The monarchy was abolished in 1946.
- In 1947 a new constitution destroyed democracy and outlawed opposition parties.

What was the Bulgaria dispute?

The Bulgaria Dispute was a crisis between Greece and Bulgaria following the killing of a Greek captain and soldier.

> **DID YOU KNOW?**
>
> **During the Cold War, the BBC employed a journalist and Bulgarian dissident called Georgi Markov.**
>
> In 1978 he was murdered in London after being injected with poison. No suspect was caught, but many believed he was assassinated by the Bulgarian secret service.

ROMANIA

'So far as Britain is concerned, how would it do for you to have 90% predominance in Romania, for us to have 90% of the say in Greece?' - Churchill to Stalin in 1944, in the so-called 'Percentages Agreement'

What is Romania?

Romania is a south-eastern European country.

When did Romania become a satellite state?

Soviet control was established in Romania in 1947.

How did Romania become a satellite state?

Romania became a satellite state through 4 key events:

- ✓ Romania was a monarchy with little support for communism. During the Second World War it was a German ally.
- ✓ Soviet troops remained there after the war. The Soviets accepted a coalition government in 1945 with communists in key positions.
- ✓ The communists gradually took over the police, and rigged elections in 1946 gave them 90% of the vote.
- ✓ The main opposition leader was subject to a 'show trial' in October 1947 and King Michael was forced to abdicate.

> **DID YOU KNOW?**
>
> **In 1945 and 1946, King Michael of Romania went on a 'royal strike' and refused to sign laws made by the communist government.**
>
> He was forced to abdicate shortly after attending the wedding of Queen Elizabeth II and Prince Philip in 1947.

YUGOSLAVIA

The leader of Yugoslavia, General Tito, was a communist but resisted control by the USSR.

 What was Yugoslavia?

Yugoslavia is a country in south east Europe. It was led by the communist Josip Tito from 1945 until his death in 1980.

 When did Yugoslavia become communist?

Yugoslavia became a communist state in 1945. It was unique amongst the countries of eastern Europe as it became communist independently and was therefore not a satellite state of the Soviet Union.

 What were relations like between Yugoslavia and the USSR?

At first, relations between Yugoslavia and the USSR were good. However, Yugoslavia's leader, Tito, repeatedly ignored Stalin as he was determined to implement communism in his own way. Things came to a head when Tito applied for Marshall Aid *(p.31)*.

 Was Yugoslavia a member of Cominform?

Yugoslavia was a member of Cominform *(p.32)* until it was expelled in 1948 due to worsening relations with the USSR.

 What was Yugoslavia's role in the Cold War?

Yugoslavia's position was unusual as the only communist state in Europe not behind the Iron Curtain. As a result, the USA gave it economic aid. However, it was a turbulent relationship as the state was too independent for the USA.

> **DID YOU KNOW?**
>
> **Yugoslavia's own version of communism was called Titoism, after its leader.**
>
> The USSR produced more negative propaganda about General Tito during the Cold War than it did about America and the west.

IRON CURTAIN SPEECH, 1946

'From Stettin in the Baltic, to Trieste in the Adriatic, an iron curtain has descended across the continent.' - Winston Churchill, 1947

What was the 'Iron Curtain' speech?

Winston Churchill *(p.76)*, although no longer the prime minister of Britain, gave a significant speech where he described how Europe had been divided by an 'iron curtain'. This analogy described the USSR's actions in eastern Europe that had divided Europe in two.

When was the 'Iron Curtain' speech delivered?

Winston Churchill *(p.76)* gave the speech in March 1946.

Who delivered the 'Iron Curtain' speech?

Winston Churchill *(p.76)* gave the 'Iron Curtain' speech.

Where was the 'Iron Curtain' speech delivered?

Winston Churchill *(p.76)* gave the speech in Fulton, USA.

What important argument was made by Churchill during the 'Iron Curtain' speech?

Churchill *(p.76)* argued that:

- ✅ Strong American-British relations were essential to stop the spread of communism and maintain peace.
- ✅ The USA must play an active role in world affairs.

Why was the 'Iron Curtain' speech important?

It helped bolster American and western European opposition to communism and the Soviet Union. It worsened relations between the USSR and the West.

How did Stalin respond to the 'Iron Curtain' speech?

Stalin responded to the 'Iron Curtain' speech by:

- ✅ Comparing Churchill *(p.76)* to Hitler and claiming Churchill was attempting to draw racial boundaries.
- ✅ Calling Churchill *(p.76)* a warmonger (someone who encourages or seeks war).

> **DID YOU KNOW?**
>
> Some regard Churchill's 'Iron Curtain' speech as the real beginning of the Cold War, because it was one of the first public announcements of hostility.
>
> The 'Iron Curtain' speech is officially named 'The Sinews of Peace'.

TRUMAN DOCTRINE, 1947

'The seeds of totalitarian regimes are nurtured by misery and want. They spread and grow in the evil soil of poverty and strife.' - Harry Truman

What was the Truman Doctrine?

The Truman Doctrine was an American policy which was anti-communist and involved the containment of communism. It led to the Marshall Plan *(p.31)*.

When did the Truman Doctrine begin?

President Harry S Truman announced his doctrine on 12th March, 1947.

Why was the Truman Doctrine established?

There were 3 main reasons the Truman Doctrine was created:

- Britain could not afford to give any more military support to the Greek government in the civil war against Greek communists.
- The USA promised $400 million in aid to Greece and Turkey to help win the war against the Greek communists.
- It aimed to contain the spread of communism by giving military and economic assistance to any country threatened by communism.

What were the main points of the Truman Doctrine?

The Truman Doctrine contained 3 key points:

- It stated the world had a choice between communism, or capitalism and democracy;
- The USA would send troops and economic aid to countries threatened by communism so it was contained and could not spread;
- The USA would no longer follow an isolationist foreign policy and would now get involved in the affairs of other countries, rather than stay out of them.

What conditions were there in order for countries to receive aid under the Truman Doctrine?

Countries had to choose capitalism over communism in order to receive aid from the USA.

What was the importance of the Truman Doctrine?

There were 4 main reasons the Truman Doctrine was important:

- It meant the USA officially abandoned its isolationist foreign policy and would play an active role in the world.
- It meant the USA was on a potential collision course with the USSR as the doctrine was directed against the spread of communism.

- ✓ It directly resulted in the creation of the Marshall Plan *(p.31)*.
- ✓ It resulted in the further deterioration in the relationship between the USA and the USSR.

> **DID YOU KNOW?**
> The Truman Doctrine was the first American policy that expressed the need to contain the spread of communism.

MARSHALL PLAN, 1947

'Our policy is directed not against any country or doctrine but against hunger, poverty, desperation and chaos.' - Harry Truman

What was the Marshall Plan?
The Marshall Plan was a scheme to provide economic aid to Europe.

When was the Marshall Plan introduced?
The Marshall Plan was introduced in 1948.

Who came up with the Marshall Plan?
It was proposed by the US Secretary of State, George C Marshall.

Why was the Marshall Plan introduced?
The Marshall Plan was essentially the Truman Doctrine *(p.30)* in action. By making countries dependent on US dollars, it would prevent the spread of communism.

How much money was provided by the Marshall Plan?
$13.3 billion was provided by the USA to help rebuild Europe.

Which countries received aid under the Marshall Plan?
A total of 16 western European countries, including France, West Germany and Britain, received aid.

What was it hoped would be achieved by the Marshall Plan?
It was feared the damage and poverty caused by the Second World War would encourage people to turn to communism. Giving countries money to rebuild would stop them becoming communist.

What were the conditions needed to receive aid from the Marshall Plan?
In order to receive money, countries had to trade with the USA and be capitalist.

What was the reaction to the Marshall Plan?
The USSR reacted in 4 main ways to the Marshall Plan:
- ✓ The Soviet Union saw both the Truman Doctrine *(p.30)* and the Marshall Plan as a threat to communism.
- ✓ Stalin called it 'dollar imperialism' and claimed the USA was trying to take over Europe using its economic strength.

- Stalin responded by creating Cominform *(p.32)* in 1947, which coordinated and controlled communist parties in Europe from the USSR.
- Comecon *(p.33)* was established in 1949 to organise economic trade between eastern Europe and the USSR.

What was the significance of the Marshall Plan?

The Marshall Plan was significant for 4 key reasons:

- It helped the economic recovery of western Europe.
- It limited the expansion of Soviet influence in Europe so the USSR was 'contained'.
- It deepened the divide between western Europe and eastern Europe as they were now divided politically and economically.
- It worsened the relationship between the USA and the USSR.

> **DID YOU KNOW?**
>
> If the USA spent the same proportion of its GDP on aid today as during the Marshall Plan, it would amount to $800 billion dollars.

COMINFORM, 1947

The Cominform described the world as divided into two sharply drawn camps - the camp of imperialism and war headed by the United States, and the camp of socialism and peace headed by the Soviet Union.

What was Cominform?

Cominform was the Communist Information Bureau. It organised all communist parties in Europe under the USSR's control.

When was Cominform created?

The Communist Information Bureau was created in September 1947.

Who were the members of Cominform?

Members included the USSR, France, Italy, Czechoslovakia, Bulgaria, Poland, Yugoslavia and Romania.

Why was Cominform created?

Cominform was created for 2 key reasons:

- It was a reaction to the creation of the Marshall Plan *(p.31)* by the USA.
- It was a way in which the USSR could control all communist parties in Europe.

Why was Cominform important?

Cominform meant that the USSR politically controlled all communist parties in eastern Europe. It created a trade network between communist countries.

> **DID YOU KNOW?**
>
> **The leader of Yugoslavia, General Tito, resisted being controlled by Cominform.**
> As a result, he was expelled from the bureau in 1948.

COMECON, 1949

Comecon was seen as the Soviet 'answer' to the Marshall Plan.

What was Comecon?

Comecon was the Council for Mutual Economic Assistance. It was the Soviet Union's alternative to the Marshall Plan *(p.31)*.

When was Comecon created?

Comecon was created in January 1949.

Who was part of Comecon?

Comecon included the Soviet Union, Bulgaria, Czechoslovakia, Poland, Romania, Hungary, Albania and the German Democratic Republic (East Germany).

Why was Comecon created?

Comecon was a reaction to the Marshall Plan *(p.31)*, introduced by the USA, and was created for 2 main reasons:

- ✓ Stalin wanted to reduce any possible economic influence the USA could have on eastern Europe's communist countries by creating his own version of the Marshall Plan *(p.31)*.
- ✓ It was a method of controlling the satellite states in eastern Europe by tying them into close trading relationships with the USSR and each other.

What was the importance of Comecon?

Comecon, with the Marshall Plan *(p.31)*, divided Europe into two economic spheres of influence; western European was capitalist and eastern European was communist.

> **DID YOU KNOW?**
>
> Comecon was used to develop closer ties between the USSR and the countries of eastern Europe.

BERLIN BLOCKADE, 1948-49
The Berlin Blockade by Stalin was designed to establish dominance over Berlin and Germany.

What was the Berlin Blockade?
The USSR closed all road, rail and river transport links into West Berlin. This stopped all supplies getting into the city. British, French and US troops were asked to leave.

When was the Berlin Blockade?
The Berlin Blockade started in June 1948 and ended in May 1949.

What caused the Berlin Blockade?
There were 8 key causes of the Berlin Blockade:
- The growing tension between the USA and the USSR over the future of Germany.
- The growing tension between the USA and the USSR because of their ideological differences and the start *(p.70)* of the Cold War *(p.16)*.
- In January 1947, the British and USA joined their zones, creating 'Bizonia'. This broke the agreements made at the Potsdam Conference *(p.21)*.
- In December 1947, at the London Conference, Britain, France and the USA met to discuss Germany and decide Germany's new constitution. The USSR was not included.
- In March 1948, France's zone joined Bizonia to create 'Trizonia'.
- The USSR left the Allied Control Commission, accusing the West of breaking the Potsdam agreements. They were angry the London Conference had taken place.
- In April 1948, Trizonia started to receive Marshall Aid *(p.31)* and began to rebuild.
- Britain, France and the USA introduced a new 'safe' currency, the Deutschmark, into Trizonia on 23rd June, 1948, which angered the USSR.

What were the consequences of the Berlin Blockade?
There were 3 main consequences of the Berlin Blockade:
- It prevented supplies reaching West Berlin.
- It led to the Berlin Airlift *(p.35)* from June 1948 to May 1949, in which the Western powers used airplanes to fly supplies into West Berlin.
- The relationship between the USSR and the West deteriorated further, eventually leading to the creation of NATO *(p.36)*.

What was the significance of the Berlin Blockade?
The Berlin Blockade was significant for 2 key reasons:
- The West saw it as an act of aggression by Stalin.
- It created the first major crisis between the USA and the USSR in the Cold War *(p.16)*.

DID YOU KNOW?

The blockade lasted 318 days (11 months).

BERLIN AIRLIFT, 1948-49
Rather than risk war over the Blockade, the Americans got around it with the Berlin Airlift.

What did the western powers do in response to the Berlin Blockade?
Western powers responded to the blockade of West Berlin by organising an airlift. Supplies were flown into West Berlin every day.

When was the Berlin Airlift?
The Berlin Airlift saw supplies flown into Berlin every day from 26th June, 1948, to 12th May, 1949.

Why did the Berlin Airlift happen?
There were 3 main reasons the Berlin Airlift occurred:
- The West did not want to be forced out of West Berlin because Stalin would be able to take over.
- The USA wanted to contain communism, as promised in the Truman Doctrine *(p.30)*.
- It was a way to get around the blockade without starting a war.

What happened during the Berlin Airlift?
There were 3 key events during the Berlin Airlift:
- Britain, France and the USA flew in supplies of food, medicine and fuel throughout the Blockade.
- By the end of the Blockade, approximately 8,000 tonnes of supplies were being flown in every day.
- A new airport called Berlin-Tegel was built and a new runway was built at Berlin-Tempelhof to cope with the number of planes flying in supplies.

What were the consequences of the Berlin Airlift?
There were 4 key consequences of the Berlin Airlift:
- Two Germanies were created; The Federal Republic of Germany (West Germany) in May 1949 and the German Democratic Republic (East Germany) in October 1949.
- It led to the USA creating a military alliance called NATO *(p.36)* in April 1949.
- Europe was divided even more: politically (capitalism versus communism), economically (Marshall Aid *(p.31)* versus Comecon *(p.33)*), and now militarily.
- The balance of power became more unstable when the USSR conducted its first successful atomic bomb test in August 1949.

DID YOU KNOW?

The Americans airlifted a total of 2,245,315 tons of supplies into Berlin during the airlift.
An Allied plane landed in Berlin every minute.

NATO, 1949

'The North Atlantic Treaty Organisation is first and foremost an effective defence alliance. It prevents potential opponents from being tempted to exert political pressure on any one of the allies through military force.' - Willy Brandt, 1968

What is NATO?
NATO is an acronym for North Atlantic Treaty Organisation. It is a military alliance based on the promise of mutual defence against an attack by an external force.

When was NATO formed?
NATO was formed on 4th April, 1949.

Who joined NATO?
The original 12 members were: the USA, Canada, Great Britain, Belgium, France, Italy, the Netherlands, Norway, Denmark, Luxembourg, Portugal and Iceland.

Why was NATO created?
NATO was formed by the USA and other western countries for 2 main reasons:
- Stalin and USSR's actions in the Berlin Blockade *(p.34)* had worried them.
- They wanted military protection from future aggression.

What were the consequences of the creation of NATO?
There were 4 key consequences of the creation of NATO:
- The USSR was contained in Europe, ensuring if it attacked any European member of NATO the other members would help the country under attack.
- All NATO members were protected by the promise of mutual military aid against any Soviet attack, helping to make the security of western Europe stronger.
- In response to West Germany joining NATO, the Soviet Union formed the Warsaw Pact *(p.37)* in 1955 so the USSR had full military control over eastern Europe.
- The USA had committed to a military presence in Europe.

What message was sent by the creation of NATO?
The creation of NATO sent 2 main messages to the USSR:
- The USA and western European countries would not accept Soviet aggression.
- The West would maintain the idea of containment set out in the Truman Doctrine *(p.30)*.

Why was NATO important?
NATO was important for 2 main reasons:
- It was based on the idea of 'collective security' - when one country is attacked, the rest must assist it.
- It acted as a deterrent *(p.54)* to a military attack by the Soviet Union on western Europe.

DID YOU KNOW?

NATO still exists today.

WARSAW PACT, 1955

After West Germany joined NATO, the Soviets hurriedly set up their own answer to the organisation - the Warsaw Pact.

What was the Warsaw Pact?
The Warsaw Pact was a defensive military alliance between the USSR and eastern European countries.

When was the Warsaw Pact signed?
The Warsaw Pact was established on 14th May, 1955.

Who was part of the Warsaw Pact?
The members of the Warsaw Pact were the USSR, Albania, Bulgaria, Czechoslovakia, East Germany, Hungary, Poland and Romania.

Why was the Warsaw Pact created?
There were 2 key reasons the Warsaw Pact was created:
- ✓ The USSR felt threatened when West Germany was allowed to join NATO *(p.36)* in 1955 because Germany had invaded Russia in both world wars.
- ✓ The Pact would increase the USSR's control over eastern Europe.

What did the members of the Warsaw Pact agree to?
By joining the Warsaw Pact, members agreed to defend each other if they were attacked by a non-member. This was the idea of collective security.

What were the consequences of the creation of the Warsaw Pact?
There were 3 main consequences of the creation of the Warsaw Pact:
- ✓ The USSR increased control over the satellite states in eastern Europe because it dominated the Pact.
- ✓ Europe was now divided politically, economically and militarily into two hostile camps.
- ✓ It intensified the arms race with the West.

> **DID YOU KNOW?**
>
> The USSR heavily prioritised the Warsaw Pact - during the Hungarian Uprising of 1956, it was the Hungarian government's attempt to leave it that provoked the Soviets to invade.

ARMS RACE

'I think the bomb instead constitutes merely a first step in a new control by man over the forces of nature too revolutionary and dangerous to fit into old concepts.' - Henry Stimson

What was the arms race?
The arms race was a competition between the USA and the USSR to gain military dominance by developing their nuclear capabilities and weapons.

When was the arms race?
The Soviet Union emerged as a nuclear power in 1949, leading to the arms race with the USA. This lasted until the end of the Cold War *(p.16)* in 1990.

What was the importance of the arms race?
The arms race was important for 2 main reasons:
- It led to the fear of mutually assured destruction as both sides had enough weapons to destroy the world many times over.
- The USA and the USSR had to find ways to solve disputes that did not result in a nuclear war.

What were the most important events of the arms race?
There were 6 main military achievements and events during the arms race:
- 1945 - the USA dropped atomic bombs on Hiroshima and Nagasaki, bringing the Second World War to an end.
- 1949 - the USSR tested an atomic bomb.
- 1952 - the USA developed the hydrogen bomb.
- 1953 - the USSR tested its own hydrogen bomb.
- 1957 - both the USA and USSR successfully tested intercontinental ballistic missiles (ICBMs).
- 1962 - the Cuban Missile Crisis *(p.46)* was the highest point of tension in the arms race.

What role did brinkmanship play in the arms race?
Brinkmanship was important in the arms race because:
- An enemy could be forced to back down in a moment of crisis by pushing it to the brink of an unwanted war.
- To make any threats credible, both sides needed nuclear weapons.
- The Cuban Missile Crisis *(p.46)* is an example of brinkmanship. The USA and the USSR were very close to a nuclear war, with both sides threatening conflict until the USSR backed down.

What was the theory of mutually assured destruction, or MAD in the arms race?
Mutually assured destruction, or MAD, was the following theory:
- It had developed by the 1960s.
- It stated that if either the USA or the USSR used their nuclear weapons, both would be destroyed. Each possessed so many, the damage would be unimaginable.
- It was believed war would be prevented because both sides feared it; a nuclear war was, in theory, unwinnable.

What was nuclear utilisation target selection in the arms race?
Nuclear utilisation target selection theory, or NUTs:
- Developed in the 1980s.
- Was a theory President Reagan believed in. He thought a limited nuclear war was possible as long as the USA struck at the USSR first and wiped out its nuclear weapons.

What were intercontinental ballistic missiles in the arms race?
Intercontinental ballistic missiles, called ICBMs, were nuclear-armed ballistic missiles with a range of more than 3,500 miles.

What were anti-ballistic missiles in the arms race?
Anti-ballistic missiles were missiles that would intercept and destroy other ballistic missiles. The USA and the USSR developed ABMs in the 1960s.

What were multiple independent reentry vehicles in the arms race?
Multiple independent reentry vehicles (MIRVs) were developed in 1968. These missiles carried multiple warheads which could each be independently targeted.

> **DID YOU KNOW?**
>
> In October 1961, the USSR tested its largest nuclear weapon, the Tsar Bomba, creating the most powerful man-made explosion ever seen.
>
> The blast waves travelled around the earth three times!

DE-STALINISATION

Khrushchev began the policy of de-Stalinisation after his 'Secret Speech' in which he criticised the brutality of Stalin's government.

What was De-Stalinisation?
De-Stalinisation was a series of political reforms in the USSR which were introduced after the death of Stalin in 1953.

When did De-Stalinisation happen?
De-Stalinisation took place from 1956 to 1964.

Who introduced De-Stalinisation?
Khrushchev brought in the policy of De-Stalinisation in his 'Secret Speech'.

What did the 'Secret Speech' say about Stalin's government during the period of De-Stalinisation?
Khrushchev's 'Secret Speech' criticised the brutality of Stalin's government and led people to believe Soviet control would be relaxed in eastern Europe.

Why was De-Stalinisation introduced?
There were 3 possible reasons why Khrushchev brought in his policy of De-Stalinisation:
- ☑ To weaken the position of his political rivals inside the USSR's Communist Party.
- ☑ To weaken the secret police and the Gulag system.
- ☑ To help develop peaceful coexistence with the USA, with the idea the USSR would not interfere in America's affairs.

What was the impact of De-Stalinisation on the Cold War?
De-Stalinisation influenced the Cold War *(p. 16)* in 3 main ways:
- ☑ It was seen as a time when the relationship between the USA and the USSR improved - there was a 'thaw' in the Cold War *(p. 16)*.

- When the contents of the 'Secret Speech' reached eastern Europe, people expected the repressive nature of communist-controlled governments would be relaxed.
- It encouraged rebellions in Hungary and, later, Czechoslovakia.

> **DID YOU KNOW?**
> Khrushchev's 'Secret Speech', in which he criticised Stalin, was considered so shocking that some listeners were said to have suffered heart attacks.
> The 'Secret Speech' soon leaked and led to demands for reform in eastern Europe.

HUNGARIAN UPRISING, 1956

'The 5,000 students ... were joined shortly after dusk by thousands of workers and others. The great crowd then marched to the Stalin monument. Ropes were wound round the statue's neck, and, to cheers, the crowd attempted to topple the statue.' - The Manchester Guardian, 1956

What was the Hungarian Uprising?
The Hungarian people demonstrated against communist rule. Prime Minister Imre Nagy ended one-party rule and announced that Hungary would leave the Warsaw Pact *(p.37)*.

When did the Hungarian Uprising happen?
The uprising in Hungary happened between July and October, 1956.

Why did the Hungarian Uprising happen?
There were 4 main causes of the Hungarian Uprising:
- Since 1949 the USSR had taken industrial and agricultural goods away from Hungary, and as a result Hungary was very poor.
- Hungary's Prime Minister, Matyas Rakosi, was a hard-line communist and had crushed all political opposition in Hungary.
- Khrushchev, the new leader of the USSR, gave a secret speech in 1956 in which he criticised Stalin's brutality. Consequently, Hungarians hoped for more freedom.
- Living standards had fallen and people were suffering.

What happened during the Hungarian Uprising?
There were 4 key events during the Hungarian Uprising:
- In July 1956, people began to protest about the repressive nature of the government and low standards of living.
- Rakosi was replaced by Gero as prime minister in the hope protests would decrease.
- In October 1956 there were huge protests by students and workers demanding more freedom which turned into riots.
- On 24th October, Nagy was appointed prime minister. He was more liberal and brought in reforms.

What reforms did Nagy want to introduce during the Hungarian Uprising?
Nagy announced 5 key reforms, including:
- Relaxing censorship.

- Allowing free elections.
- Allowing non-communists into the government.
- A proposal for Hungary to withdraw from the Warsaw Pact (p.37).
- The release of political prisoners, including Cardinal Jozsef Mindszenty who had been imprisoned by Rakosi.

Why did the USSR invade Hungary during the Hungarian Uprising?

The USSR invaded Hungary because of Nagy's reforms and specifically because Nagy proposed that Hungary withdraw from the Warsaw Pact (p.37).

What happened as a consequence of the Hungarian Uprising?

There were 9 important consequences of the Hungarian Uprising:

- On 4th November, 1956, Khrushchev and the politburo ordered Soviet forces to invade Hungary with 200,000 troops to remove Nagy and crush the uprising.
- Between 20,000 and 30,000 Hungarians were killed.
- 1,000 Soviet troops died.
- 200,000 Hungarians became refugees.
- Nagy's government was deported, and Nagy was executed.
- Nagy was replaced by Janos Kadar and a new pro-Communist government loyal to the USSR was set up.
- All Nagy's reforms were reversed.
- This was used as a warning to other dissenting (protesting) countries in eastern Europe.
- It increased tension between the West and the East.

What was the response of the West to the Hungarian Uprising?

The West responded in 4 key ways:

- The United Nations condemned the Soviet actions.
- Spain, the Netherlands and Switzerland boycotted the 1956 Olympics.
- America accepted 80,000 refugees from Hungary.
- The USA could not send troops to help Hungary because the Warsaw Pact (p.37) would see it as an invasion and war would break out.

What did the new government do after the Hungarian Uprising?

The new Hungarian government, under Janos Kadar, remained under Soviet control and reacted in 3 key ways:

- It stamped out remaining resistance. 35,000 Hungarian protesters were arrested and 300 executed.
- A few of the reforms demanded by the Hungarians were introduced, cautiously.
- Kadar remained firmly in favour of Hungary's membership of the Warsaw Pact (p.37).

What was the importance of the Hungarian Uprising?

The Hungarian Uprising was important because it affected the relationship between the USA and the USSR in 3 key ways:

- The USA supported the uprising but could not interfere, so now looked weak.
- Khrushchev's position was strengthened as a result.
- The USSR and the USA's relationship deteriorated because the USA had condemned the USSR's actions, increasing tension.

> **DID YOU KNOW?**
> The crushing of the 1956 uprising by the Soviets caused several of the most famous members of communist parties around the world to leave in disgust.

BERLIN CRISIS, 1958-61

The Berlin Crisis was the culmination of conflict between the USSR and USA over the future of Germany.

What was the Berlin Crisis?

The Berlin Crisis concerned the occupational status of the city and the numbers of East Germans fleeing to West Berlin, said to be some 2.7 million people. Khrushchev delivered an ultimatum, demanding foreign troops withdraw within a period of 6 months.

When did the Berlin Crisis happen?

The Berlin Crisis took place between 1957 and 1961.

Why did people move to West Berlin during the Berlin Crisis?

For many East Germans, life in the West seemed more attractive for 3 key reasons:

- Wages were higher in West Berlin.
- West Berliners had more freedom and more variety in the goods that they could buy.
- The Allies poured money into West Berlin, so that the contrast between the affluence of the city's two sides was more obvious.

How was the economy affected during the Berlin Crisis?

The West German economy benefitted from skilled labourers, while the East suffered a skills shortage.

What were the key events of the Berlin Crisis?

There were 8 key events during the Berlin Crisis:

- In 1958 the leader of East Germany, Walter Ulbricht, asked Khrushchev, the leader of the USSR, to help stop East Germans from fleeing to the west.
- In November 1958, Khrushchev issued his ultimatum demanding Western troops withdraw from West Berlin.
- In 1959, Khrushchev and President Eisenhower met in Geneva to discuss the Berlin Crisis, which resulted in Khrushchev withdrawing his ultimatum.
- A second summit, at Camp David in America in 1959, did not result in a solution.
- In 1960, a US spy plane was shot down by the Soviets.
- President Eisenhower refused to apologise for the U2 spy plane so Khrushchev left the Paris Conference of 1960. Again, this meant no solution was found to the Berlin Crisis.
- In 1961, the US and the USSR met again in Vienna. Khrushchev reissued his ultimatum for the Western powers to withdraw their troops from Berlin within 6 months.
- President Kennedy *(p.80)* began to prepare for war, increasing American defence spending by $3.5 billion. The USSR did the same.

What were the results of the Berlin Crisis?

There were 6 key results:

- East German troops began to build the Berlin Wall *(p.43)* on 13th August, 1961.
- By October 1961 West Berlin was entirely shut off from East Germany. Initially, foreigners could cross into East Berlin through a US Army checkpoint, known as Checkpoint Charlie.
- It reduced tension as the crisis was solved without going to war.
- French, British and American troops remained in West Berlin.
- It was a propaganda victory for the West and a humiliation for the USSR, because the East had to build a wall to prevent its people fleeing.
- As the USSR had been humiliated, Khrushchev became more determined to win the Cuban Missile Crisis *(p.46)* in 1962.

> **DID YOU KNOW?**
> The flight of East German refugees to the West is often referred to as a 'brain drain' because it was mainly well-educated professionals who fled.

THE BERLIN WALL, 1961-62

The Berlin Wall is arguably the first symbol that comes to mind when people think of the Cold War.

What was the Berlin Wall?

The Berlin Wall, built by East Germany, divided East and West Berlin. It was constructed of concrete slabs in the city centre and barbed wire fences around the outer edges.

 When was the Berlin Wall built?

The building of the Berlin Wall began on the 12th-13th August, 1961.

 Why was the Berlin Wall built?

There were 2 main reasons for the building of the Berlin Wall:

- To prevent East German people defecting to West Berlin.
- To keep capitalism and spies from the West out, according to the Soviets and East German government.

 What were the consequences of the Berlin Wall being built?

There were 7 key consequences of the building of the Berlin Wall:

- It solved the refugee crisis for East Germany, which now controlled who could leave and enter East Berlin.
- West Berlin remained under Allied control, making it harder for the Soviets to control the whole of East Germany.
- The number of military alerts in Berlin decreased as the situation there became less tense.
- It was a humiliation for the USSR and a propaganda victory for the West, as it appeared a wall was needed to prevent people fleeing.
- It divided West Berliners from East Berliners. Families and friends were separated for years.
- At least 140 people died attempting to cross the Berlin Wall from the east to the west between 1961 and 1989; some reports say the figure was higher.

- ☑ It became an iconic symbol of the Cold War *(p. 16)*.

What was President Kennedy's response to the building of the Berlin Wall?
President Kennedy's *(p.80)* responded in 2 main ways:
- ☑ He said: 'It's not a very nice solution but a wall is a hell of a lot better than a war.'.
- ☑ He visited West Berlin in June 1963, where he gave the 'Ich bin ein Berliner' speech to show his support for West Berliners.

What was the impact of the Berlin Wall on the relationship between the USA and the USSR?
There were both positive and negative effects on the relationship between the USA and the USSR:
- ☑ It solved the crisis over Berlin so reduced tension.
- ☑ There were fewer military alerts in Berlin as the situation had stabilised.
- ☑ Germany had been a source of conflict between the USSR and the USA since 1945. Their relationship had deteriorated so much a wall had to be built.
- ☑ It created a long-lasting symbol of the Cold War *(p.16)* which signified the divide between the two sides.
- ☑ Khrushchev had suffered a humiliating defeat so decided to place missiles in Cuba to show he could stand up to the USA.
- ☑ Khrushchev saw Kennedy *(p.80)* as weak as he had not stopped the wall from being built.

What happened at Checkpoint Charlie after the Berlin Wall was built?
Two main points should be noted about what happened at Checkpoint Charlie:
- ☑ There was an 18-hour standoff when Soviet tanks stopped Americans crossing the border on 27th-28th October, 1961.
- ☑ It was a high point of tension between East and West until an agreement between the USA and USSR ended the incident.

> **DID YOU KNOW?**
> A trapeze artist called Horst Klein managed to escape over the Berlin Wall by tightrope walking across a power line in 1962. He fell and broke both his arms, but landed in West Berlin.

CUBAN REVOLUTION, 1959
'A revolution is not a bed of roses. A revolution is a struggle to the death between the future and the past.' - Fidel Castro

What was the Cuban Revolution?
Fidel Castro led an armed uprising to bring down the dictatorship of the Cuban president, General Fulgencio Batista.

When was the Cuban Revolution?
The Cuban Revolution started in July 1953. Batista was removed from power on 31st December, 1958.

Who started the Cuban Revolution?
Fidel Castro started the Cuban Revolution.

How did the Cuban Revolution affect Cuba's relationship with the USA?
Before 1959, the USA supported Batista and there was co-operation between the two countries. This ended when diplomatic relations were broken off in January 1961.

What was the USA's reaction to the Cuban Revolution?
The USA reacted in 7 key ways:
- It wanted Cuba back inside America's sphere of influence.
- In 1959, it refused to accept compensation offered by Cuba for American-owned property and land taken in the revolution.
- Although America did recognise Castro's government, when he requested economic aid in 1960 this was denied. Instead, President Eisenhower reduced US imports of Cuban sugar by 95%.
- It supported Cuban exiles to undermine the new government.
- It refused to buy Cuban sugar, which made up a large part of the national income, and eventually ended all trade with Cuba in October 1960.
- The CIA tried unsuccessfully to assassinate Castro.
- The CIA convinced President Kennedy (p.80) that the USA needed to invade Cuba.

What became of Cuba's relationship with the USSR after the Cuban Revolution?
There were 3 important developments in Cuba's relationship with the Soviet Union:
- Cuba began to build economic links with the Soviet Union instead of the USA.
- In February 1960, it began to trade Cuban sugar for Soviet oil.
- Cuba wanted the Soviets' military defence and support.

> **DID YOU KNOW?**
> The Communist Party still rules in Cuba today.

BAY OF PIGS, 1961
The Bay of Pigs was one of the most catastrophic foreign policy interventions in American history.

What happened at the Bay of Pigs in Cuba?
The Bay of Pigs incident involved Cuban exiles, supported by US forces, invading Cuba.

When was the attack at the Bay of Pigs?
The invasion of Cuba at the Bay of Pigs took place on 17th April, 1961.

Who led the attack at the Bay of Pigs?
Cuban exiles, trained and supported by America, invaded Cuba at the Bay of Pigs.

What happened during the invasion of the Bay of Pigs?
There were 4 key events during the invasion of the Bay of Pigs:

- Castro learned about the invasion in advance because the planes were recognised as American from photographs.
- The 1,400 US-backed Cuban exiles were met by an army of 20,000 Cubans.
- The US-backed Cuban exiles surrendered.
- Almost all of those in the Cuban exile army were jailed or shot.

 What were the consequences of the attack at the Bay of Pigs?

There were 5 important consequences of the attack at the Bay of Pigs:

- The incident meant USA-Cuban relations deteriorated while Soviet-Cuban relations improved.
- Fidel Castro stayed in power.
- The USA was totally discredited because it had supported illegal acts. President Kennedy (p.80) was embarrassed and his position was weakened.
- In December 1961, Castro stated he and his government were communist.
- Castro asked Khrushchev for military support in case of future attacks by the USA.

 Why did the invasion at the Bay of Pigs fail?

There were 2 main reasons why the invasion at the Bay of Pigs failed:

- The CIA underestimated the strength of the Cubans, who had 20,000 troops and modern tanks and weapons.
- They also failed to gain the support of the Cuban people, which they assumed they would get.

> **DID YOU KNOW?**
> **The failure of the Bay of Pigs invasion had several consequences.**
> President Kennedy was humiliated, and there were a number of failed attempts by the CIA to assassinate Fidel Castro.

CUBAN MISSILE CRISIS, OCTOBER 1962

'We're eyeball to eyeball...and I think the other fellow just blinked.' - Secretary of State Dean Rusk, October 1962

 What was the Cuban Missile Crisis?

The Cuban Missile Crisis, between the USSR and the USA, was one of the most serious Cold War (p.16) crises. It happened because the USSR placed missiles in Cuba and was the closest the world had been to a possible nuclear war.

 When did the Cuban Missile Crisis happen?

The Cuban Missile Crisis lasted for 13 days, from 14th to 28th October, 1962.

 Why did the Cuban Missile Crisis happen?

6 important causes of the Cuban Missile Crisis were:

- The long-term deterioration of the relationship between the USA and Cuba, accelerated by the Cuban Revolution (p.44) in 1959 and the Bay of Pigs incident in 1961.
- This pushed Cuba closer to the USSR, which bought Cuban sugar. In return, the Cubans bought oil from the Soviets.
- Castro had declared himself a Marxist in December 1961.

- Khrushchev was concerned about the missile gap and the fact the USA had nuclear missiles based in Turkey which could easily reach the USSR.
- The immediate cause was the deployment of Soviet nuclear missiles to Cuba for protection against possible attack by the USA.
- Cuba is only 160km south of the US state of Florida, which meant the mainland was within range of any missiles placed on Cuba. The USA therefore felt threatened.

What happened during the Cuban Missile Crisis?

There were 9 key events during the crisis in October 1962:

- On 14th October, American spy planes spotted missile bases being built on Cuba.
- On 16th October, Kennedy (p.80) was informed of the missile build-up and Ex-Comm, an advisory group, was formed.
- On 20th October, Kennedy (p.80) decided to blockade Cuba. This was a 500-mile naval 'quarantine' with the aim of preventing the Soviets bringing in further military supplies or missiles.
- On 24th October, Khrushchev stated the USSR would launch nuclear missiles if America went to war in Cuba.
- The blockade began. When Soviet ships approached the blockade, some stopped and some turned around.
- On 26th October, Kennedy (p.80) received a letter from Khrushchev who offered to negotiate if the blockade was removed and the USA did not invade Cuba.
- On 27th October, Kennedy (p.80) received a second letter from Khrushchev which offered to remove the missiles if the USA removed its missiles in Turkey.
- Kennedy's (p.80) brother, Robert, negotiated with the Russian ambassador and accepted the offer on condition the removal of missiles from Turkey was kept secret.
- On 28th October, Khrushchev agreed to the dismantling of the nuclear missiles.

How was the Cuban Missile Crisis solved?

The Cuban Missile Crisis was solved because:

- Khrushchev agreed to remove missiles from Cuba if the USA removed its warheads from Italy and Turkey.
- The USA would only agree to the deal if the removal of its missiles from Italy and Turkey was kept secret.

What were the results of the Cuban Missile Crisis?

There were 6 main consequences to the Cuban Missile Crisis:

- Cuba survived as a communist country.
- Kennedy (p.80) assured the world that the USA would never invade Cuba and his public image improved.
- The Soviet Union looked weak because the world did not know the USA had removed its missiles from Turkey.
- Khrushchev lost power in the USSR and was dismissed in 1964.
- China criticised the USSR over its actions because the Soviets had made the communist world look weak. China's relationship with the USSR deteriorated.
- The USA's NATO (p.36) allies in Europe were horrified because they had not been consulted. France reacted by leaving NATO in 1966.

How did the Cuban Missile Crisis affect the relationship between the USA and the USSR?

The Cuban Missile Crisis had 2 main effects on the relationship between the USA and the USSR:

- The relationship had deteriorated almost to the brink of nuclear war, so Kennedy (p.80) wanted to focus more on the two nations' 'common interests'.
- A hotline (p.48) was set up in June 1963 between the USA and the USSR. This would help avoid crises by enabling direct and quick communication.

Why was the Cuban Missile Crisis important?
The Cuban Missile Crisis was important for 2 main reasons:
- It was the most dangerous Cold War (p.16) confrontation between the USA and the USSR and almost led to nuclear war.
- It resulted in both countries working to improve their relationship and slow down the arms race.

What nuclear treaties were signed after The Cuban Missile Crisis?
There were 3 important nuclear treaties signed after the Cuban Missile Crisis:
- 1963 - the Limited Test Ban Treaty (p.49) banned the testing of nuclear weapons in air or underwater.
- 1967 - the Outer Space Treaty (p.49) banned testing or using nuclear weapons in space.
- 1968 - the Nuclear Non-Proliferation Treaty stated the ultimate goal was world nuclear disarmament.

> **DID YOU KNOW?**
> **One man, Vasili Arkhipov, is credited with 'saving the world' by refusing to fire nuclear missiles during the crisis.**
> His actions may have prevented an all-out nuclear war. The crisis is often seen as the closest the human race has ever come to self-annihilation, with both superpowers ready to resort to a potential nuclear war.

HOTLINE, 1963
'Must a world be lost for want of a telephone call?' - Jess Gorkin, 1960

What was the hotline?
The hotline was a teleprinter set up between Washington in the USA and Moscow in the USSR as a way of providing direct communication between the White House and the Kremlin.

When was the hotline set up?
The hotline was set up in June 1963.

Why was the hotline set up?
The hotline was set up as a result of the 1962 Cuban Missile Crisis (p.46). Leaders of the USA and the USSR had been unable to communicate directly during the crisis, relying on letters and messages.

Why was the hotline important?
The hotline was important for 2 main reasons:
- It meant the USA and USSR could directly communicate with each other so in a crisis they would hopefully solve the issue more quickly.
- It was a sign that the two superpowers were attempting to improve their relationship.

DID YOU KNOW?

The hotline was a teleprinter. It has never been a telephone, as shown in some movies.

Lyndon B Johnson was the first president to use the hotline. This was in 1967 during the Six Day War in the Middle East.

LIMITED TEST BAN TREATY, 1963

The Limited Test Ban Treaty was the first attempt to slow down the arms race.

What was the Limited Test Ban Treaty?
The Limited Nuclear Test Ban Treaty banned the testing of nuclear weapons underwater, in the atmosphere or in outer space.

When was the Limited Test Ban Treaty signed?
The Limited Nuclear Test Ban Treaty was signed on 5th August, 1963.

Who signed the Limited Test Ban Treaty?
The USA, USSR and Great Britain signed the Limited Nuclear Test Ban Treaty.

Why was the Limited Test Ban Treaty important?
The Limited Test Ban Treaty was seen as an important first step in slowing down the arms race by controlling the development of nuclear weapons.

DID YOU KNOW?

The USSR and the USA were so concerned about how close they had come to nuclear war in the Cuban Missile Crisis they were now prepared to put some limits on the arms race.

OUTER SPACE TREATY, 1967

The Outer Space Treaty prevents space being weaponised.

What was the Outer Space Treaty?
The Outer Space Treaty was an agreement to not deploy nuclear weapons in space or on any other space body, or to station them in outer space. The moon would be used for peaceful purposes only.

When was the Outer Space Treaty signed?
The Outer Space Treaty was signed on 27th January, 1967.

Who signed the Outer Space Treaty?
The Outer Space Treaty was signed by the USA, USSR and Britain.

Why was the Outer Space Treaty important?
The Outer Space Treaty sets out the basic legal framework for international space law. It prevented the arms race from spreading to space.

DID YOU KNOW?
The terms of the Outer Space Treaty would have been broken by President Reagan's SDI programme.

NUCLEAR NON-PROLIFERATION TREATY, 1968

The Nuclear Non-Proliferation Treaty, 1968 was essentially about preventing the sharing of nuclear secrets.

What was the Non-Proliferation of Nuclear Weapons Treaty?
The countries that signed the Non-Proliferation of Nuclear Weapons Treaty agreed to stop the spread of nuclear weapons by not sharing their nuclear technology with other countries. The treaty is also known as the Non-Proliferation Treaty or NPT.

When was the Non-Proliferation of Nuclear Weapons Treaty signed?
The Non-Proliferation of Nuclear Weapons Treaty was signed on 1st July, 1968.

Who signed the Non-Proliferation of Nuclear Weapons Treaty?
The NPT was signed by the Soviet Union, the United Kingdom, and the United States.

DID YOU KNOW?
The 50th anniversary of the signing of the Nuclear Non-Proliferation Treaty was on 5th March, 2020.

The treaty has been vital to preventing the proliferation of nuclear weapons but has been tested by North Korea's withdrawal in 2003 and other nations acquiring nuclear status, including India and Pakistan.

PRAGUE SPRING, 1968

'I have worked for 30 years in the Party, and my whole family has devoted everything to the affairs of the Party, the affairs of socialism. Let whatever is going to happen to me happen. I'm expecting the worst for myself and I'm resigned to it.' - Alexander Dubček

What was the Prague Spring?
The Prague Spring is the term used for the brief period when the government of Czechoslovakia wanted to democratise the nation and reduce the control the USSR had on the country.

When was the Prague Spring?
The Prague Spring took place between 5th January and 21st August in 1968.

Who was responsible for the Prague Spring?
Alexander Dubček, the new leader of Czechoslovakia, introduced the reforms.

What were the causes of the Prague Spring?
There were 6 main reasons for the Prague Spring.
- Since 1957, Czechoslovakia had been led by Antonin Novotný, who was very unpopular because he was a hard-line communist.
- Novotný did not bring in reforms, despite Khrushchev's de-Stalinisation *(p.39)* policy.
- By the 1960s, the Czech economy was struggling, and the standard of living was decreasing.
- When the leader of the USSR, Brezhnev, visited Czechoslovakia in December 1967, he withdrew his support for Novotný because he was so unpopular.
- Novotný was replaced by Dubček as the leader of Czechoslovakia on 5th January, 1968, in the hope that this would reduce discontent.
- Dubček wanted to reform communism to create 'socialism with a human face'. This would enable the public to be more involved in the government and, hopefully, increase support for communism.

What were the reforms of the Prague Spring introduced by Dubček?
Dubček brought in 7 main reforms.
- Censorship was relaxed in April 1968, which allowed more criticism of communism.
- Free speech was allowed.
- Political parties other than the Communist Party were allowed to exist.
- Work councils were set up to represent workers and improve working conditions.
- The secret police had their powers restricted, so their ability to arrest and detain people without trial was reduced.
- Some capitalist elements were even allowed, to create a form of 'market socialism' economy.
- Travel restrictions were lifted, so Czechs could travel abroad.

What was the response from the Czechoslovakian Communist Party to the Prague Spring?
The response from the leaders of the Czechoslovakian Communist Party was not enthusiastic.
- Many were horrified at Dubček's reforms, believing they were a threat to communism.
- On 3rd August, 1968, 5 leading opponents of the Prague Spring reforms sent a letter to Brezhnev, outlining their concerns and asking him to intervene.

Why were Eastern Bloc leaders concerned during the Prague Spring?

Brezhnev, the leader of the USSR, and Erich Honecker, the leader of East Germany, were very worried for 3 main reasons.

- Romania would not attend Warsaw Pact *(p.37)* meetings.
- Tito, the leader of Yugoslavia, did not want the USSR to control his country.
- They feared the Prague Spring would lead to calls for reform elsewhere in the Soviet Union's sphere of influence.

What was Brezhnev's response to the Prague Spring?

Brezhnev and the Eastern Bloc responded in 12 main ways.

- In July 1968, the USSR claimed to know of plans by West Germany to invade the Sudetenland, and asked to send Soviet troops to protect Czechoslovakia. Dubček refused.
- The USSR considered economic sanctions for Czechoslovakia, but didn't want the country to seek help from the West.
- In July, the entire Soviet Politburo (cabinet) visited Czechoslovakia, to put pressure on Dubček to reverse the reforms.
- Warsaw Pact *(p.37)* troops from the USSR, Poland and East Germany completed manoeuvres in Czechoslovakia in the summer, to put more pressure on Dubček.
- On 15th July, members of the Warsaw Pact *(p.37)* sent a letter to Dubček, warning him that the reforms were dangerous to the Eastern Bloc.
- On 20th-21st August, 1968, 500,000 Soviet-led Warsaw Pact *(p.37)* troops entered Prague to arrest the reformers.
- Nobody in Czechoslovakia was expecting an invasion, especially their armed troops, who were completely unprepared.
- Dubček and other leaders were arrested. They were taken to Moscow to meet Brezhnev.
- Dubček was forced to sign the Moscow Protocol, which stated that Czechoslovakia would protect communism and the reforms would be reversed.
- All the reforms were reversed when Dubček returned to Czechoslovakia.
- In August 1968, the Brezhnev Doctrine *(p.53)* was created. The USSR had the right to invade any country in its sphere of influence which threatened the stability of eastern Europe.
- The USSR wanted to ensure it had full control over Czechoslovakia. In 1969, therefore, it replaced Dubček with Husak, a hard-line and reliable communist.

What was the reaction of the West to the Prague Spring and the Soviet invasion?

The West reacted in 3 key ways.

- The UN wanted to condemn the invasion of Czechoslovakia by Warsaw Pact *(p.37)* troops, but the USSR vetoed it.
- The USA and the West condemned the invasion.
- However, the USA did nothing because it was distracted by Vietnam, there was a US presidential election, and it was the beginning of détente. *(p.54)*

What was the reaction of the communist world to the Prague Spring and the Soviet invasion?

The communist world reacted in 5 main ways.

- Communists in western countries condemned the invasion, and created their own version of communism called Eurocommunism.
- In France and Italy, the Communist Party condemned the USSR's actions.
- Yugoslavia and Romania spoke out against the USSR's invasion, which worsened their relationship with the Soviet Union.
- Poland and East Germany were very supportive of the invasion, as they were trying to control reformers in their own countries.

- Communist China condemned the USSR invasion of Czechoslovakia, and the relationship between the two countries greatly deteriorated.

 What was the importance of the Prague Spring?

The Prague Spring and the invasion by Soviet troops were important for 3 key reasons.

- They led to the creation of the Brezhnev Doctrine (p.53), which increased USSR control over eastern Europe.
- It split the communist world, as communist parties in western Europe became independent of the USSR's control, and communist China condemned the invasion.
- It highlighted that, while the USA would condemn the USSR's actions, it wouldn't take any steps to stop them.

> **DID YOU KNOW?**
>
> Dubček believed Lenin, the first leader of the Soviet Union, had been wrong about some things and that allowing some elements of capitalism was necessary.

BREZHNEV DOCTRINE, 1968

'When forces that are hostile to socialism try to turn the development of some socialist country towards capitalism, it becomes not only a problem of the country concerned, but a common problem and concern of all socialist countries.'

 What was the Brezhnev Doctrine?

The Brezhnev Doctrine stated that the USSR had the right to invade any country in its sphere of influence which threatened the stability of eastern Europe.

 Who was behind the Brezhnev Doctrine?

Leonid Brezhnev, the leader of the USSR between 1964 and 1982, created the Brezhnev Doctrine.

 Why was the Brezhnev Doctrine introduced?

Brezhnev introduced the Brezhnev Doctrine after the Prague Spring (p.51) because he realised he could not allow reforms in other eastern European nations.

 When was the Brezhnev Doctrine created?

The Brezhnev Doctrine was created in September 1968.

 How did the West react to the Brezhnev Doctrine?

The West reacted to the Brezhnev Doctrine in 3 main ways:

- It was condemned by the USA.
- Communist parties in the democratic west were shocked and broke away from the Soviet Communist Party to create their own version of communism, called Eurocommunism.
- It was condemned by the UN.

 How did the communists react to the Brezhnev Doctrine?

Other communist states reacted in the 3 main ways to the Brezhnev Doctrine:

- ✅ Communist governments in East Germany and Poland welcomed it because they were attempting to control reformers in their own countries.
- ✅ Romania and Yugoslavia were horrified and tried to distance themselves from the USSR and be more independent.
- ✅ China was angered and insulted by the Brezhnev Doctrine, as it only gave the USSR the right to intervene. Their relationship deteriorated.

 What was the significance of the Brezhnev Doctrine for eastern Europe?

Countries in the eastern European bloc now had to obey strict Soviet rule or risk invasion.

> **DID YOU KNOW?**
> Brezhnev enjoyed receiving medals so much that he awarded himself 100 of them while in power.

DÉTENTE

'One has to be broad-minded and tolerant enough to understand the possibility and the desirability of coexistence and cooperation between nations that are vastly different in their social systems, political institutions, values, sympathies and antipathies.' - Georgi Arbatov, Soviet Central committee member, 1983

 What was détente?

Détente refers to a period during the Cold War *(p.16)* where tensions between the USA and the Soviet Union were eased. There was increased cooperation and several attempts were made to slow down the arms race.

 When did détente happen?

Détente was between 1967 and 1979.

 What role did Henry Kissinger play in détente?

Henry Kissinger was very important to détente in 3 key ways:

- ✅ As President Nixon's security advisor, he organised Nixon's trips to Moscow and China in 1972.
- ✅ He also played an important role in the SALT I *(p.55)* talks.
- ✅ As Secretary of State, Kissinger helped end the Vietnam War for which he jointly received the Nobel Peace Prize in 1973.

 Why was the policy of détente introduced?

Détente occurred for 7 key reasons:

- ✅ Both the USSR and the USA wanted to ease tensions after the Cuban Missile Crisis *(p.46)* because they came so close to nuclear war.
- ✅ The Sino-Soviet relationship had deteriorated and the USSR wanted to prevent the USA becoming closer to China. The Soviets were worried when President Nixon visited China in 1972.
- ✅ Brezhnev, the leader of the USSR, wanted an improved relationship with the USA as he wanted access to US technology and grain.
- ✅ Both sides wanted to slow down the arms race because it was very expensive and they needed the money for domestic issues.

- ✅ The USA had domestic problems with anti-Vietnam War demonstrations, race riots and massive social inequality. It needed to cut defence spending so it could invest at home.
- ✅ The USSR had economic problems and needed to cut defence spending so there was money to invest at home.
- ✅ The USA needed the USSR's help to end the Vietnam War as they were supplying the Vietnamese communists. To find a solution, the USA asked the USSR for help.

What were the key events of détente?

The 9 key events of détente were:

- ✅ 1968: Nuclear Non-Proliferation Treaty.
- ✅ 1970: Relations between East Germany and West Germany improved with the policy of Ostpolitik.
- ✅ 1970: Ostpolitik resulted in the Treaty of Warsaw, which recognised the existing borders between the countries.
- ✅ 1972: SALT 1 (p.55).
- ✅ 1972: President Nixon visited China to meet Chairman Mao and visited Brezhnev in Moscow.
- ✅ 1972: Ostpolitik continued with the signing of the Basic Treaty which established formal relations between the two German nations.
- ✅ 1973: Brezhnev, leader of the USSR, visited Washington to meet Nixon.
- ✅ 1975: Helsinki Accords and the Apollo-Soyuz Missions.
- ✅ 1979: SALT 2 (p.58).

What role did Ostpolitik play in détente?

Ostpolitik was the policy of Chancellor Willy Brandt of West Germany which aimed to reduce tensions between the two German nations.

What was the importance of détente?

The move towards détente led to the signing of the Strategic Arms Limitation Treaties, or SALT. These treaties were intended to limit the arms race in strategic ballistic missiles armed with nuclear weapons.

Why did détente end?

The main reason détente ended was due to the USSR's invasion of Afghanistan in December 1979.

DID YOU KNOW?

The word 'détente' is French and means 'easing of tension'.

SALT 1, 1972

The Strategic Arms Limitation Talks were the first concrete steps taken to control and reduce the arms race.

What was SALT 1?

The Strategic Arms Limitation Treaty, or SALT 1, was an agreement between the superpowers to limit their number of nuclear weapons.

When was SALT 1 signed?

SALT 1 was signed on 26th May, 1972.

Who signed SALT 1?

The SALT 1 agreement was signed between Richard Nixon and Leonid Brezhnev.

What was agreed in SALT 1?

There were 4 important agreements in SALT 1:

- The Anti-Ballistic Missile Treaty: anti-ballistic missiles (ABMs) were allowed at only two sites, with 100 missiles at each.
- The Interim Treaty: limited the number of intercontinental ballistic missiles (ICBMs) and submarine launched cruise missiles (SLBMs) the USA and USSR could have. The USA was allowed 1054 ICBMs, and the USSR 1618.
- There would be a five-year delay in building more missiles, so another treaty (SALT 2 *(p.58)*) would have to be negotiated at the end of that time.
- The Basic Principles Agreement: established what the USA and USSR would do to avoid nuclear war breaking out and the rules if it did occur.

What were the limitations of SALT 1?

SALT 1 was limited in 3 main ways because:

- It did not cover intermediate-range nuclear weapons, which were still being deployed by both countries.
- It did not include multiple independently targeted reentry vehicles (MIRVs) which carried multiple warheads on a single missile.
- Although it slowed down the arms race, both sides still had enough nuclear missiles to destroy the planet and there was no agreement to not use those missiles.

Why was SALT 1 important?

SALT 1 was important because of 3 key reasons:

- It slowed the arms race.
- It showed an improvement in relations between the USA and the Soviet Union.
- It led to further improvements such as the Helsinki Conference *(p.57)* in 1975 and the SALT 2 *(p.58)* negotiations.

DID YOU KNOW?

Gerard Smith was the lead US negotiator at the Strategic Arms Limitation Talks.

His opening comment at the talks was, 'The limitation of strategic arms is in the mutual interests of our country and the Soviet Union.'

HELSINKI ACCORDS, 1975

The Helsinki Conference led to increased cooperation between the superpowers.

What was the Helsinki Conference?
The Helsinki Conference focused on security and co-operation in Europe. The agreements made there are known as the Helsinki Accords.

Where was the Helsinki Conference?
It was held in Helsinki, Finland.

When was the Helsinki Conference?
The Helsinki Conference took place from July 1973 to August 1975.

Who signed the treaties at the Helsinki Conference?
The agreements were signed by the USA, Canada, the Soviet Union, and all European countries excluding Albania and Andorra.

Why was the Helsinki Conference held?
The Helsinki Conference was held in an effort to reduce tensions between the Soviet and Western blocs.

How were the agreements split at the Helsinki Conference?
The agreements of the Helsinki Conference were split into 3 main 'baskets':
- ☑ Basket 1: The current borders of European countries could not be changed or violated. No country could interfere in the affairs of another country. All disputes would be solved peacefully.
- ☑ Basket 2: Promoted trade between the East and West (the USA would buy USSR's oil; the USSR would buy the USA's wheat). There would be scientific and educational cooperation.
- ☑ Basket 3: To respect human rights such as freedom of speech and free movement.

What was the problem with the agreements made at the Helsinki Conference?
There were 2 main problems with the agreements made at the Helsinki Conference:
- ☑ The Soviet Union continued to apply the Brezhnev Doctrine *(p.53)* in eastern Europe, and anyone who opposed it was treated severely.
- ☑ In reality, the Eastern Bloc countries did not uphold the human rights agreement.

DID YOU KNOW?

One key consequence of the Helsinki Accords was the Apollo-Soyuz Mission.

'Basket 2' of the agreement was to increase cooperation and this resulted in the joint space mission.

APOLLO-SOYUZ MISSION, 1975

The Apollo-Soyuz Space Mission was the first time the USSR and the USA cooperated on a space mission.

What was the Apollo-Soyuz mission?
The Apollo-Soyuz mission was a joint mission between the USA and the USSR. Their crafts docked in space and the astronauts shook hands.

When was the Apollo-Soyuz mission?
The Apollo-Soyuz mission happened in July 1975.

What was the significance of the Apollo-Soyuz mission?
The Apollo-Soyuz mission was significant because it was the first time the USSR and USA had cooperated in space rather than competing. It was a sign of détente. *(p.54)*

> **DID YOU KNOW?**
>
> During the space mission, the astronauts were given a tour of each other's space craft and completed some science experiments.

SALT 2, 1979

The Strategic Arms Limitation Talks 2 would have paved the way for further steps to control and reduce the arms race.

What was SALT 2?
The Strategic Arms Limitations Talks 2 was the second round of talks to limit the use of multi-warhead missiles and the creation of new launch stations.

When was SALT 2 signed?
SALT 2 was signed in June 1979, but it was not ratified by the US Senate so did not become official US policy.

Who signed SALT 2?
SALT 2 was signed in Vienna, Austria, by President Jimmy Carter and General Secretary Leonid Brezhnev.

What was agreed in SALT 2?
There were 3 main terms:

- ✔ There would be further reductions in nuclear weapons until 1985, which would limit the number of long-range missiles.
- ✔ The USA and USSR would have an equal limit of 2,400 in the number of missile launchers and also in strategic bombs (ICBMs, SLBMs and heavy bombers).
- ✔ New types of ICBMs were banned from being tested or deployed.

What were the reactions to SALT 2?
Reactions to Salt 2 were negative overall, with most western politicians uncertain about the treaty in 2 key ways:
- ☑ Some US politicians thought SALT 2 gave too much to the Soviet Union, and it was never ratified in the USA.
- ☑ West German politicians believed it made the USA less likely to use nuclear weapons to protect West Germany.

What were the limitations of SALT 2?
The limits imposed on the number of missiles did not reduce the overall numbers each country had.

What happened to SALT 2?
There were 3 main events which affected SALT 2:
- ☑ Diplomatic relations between the USA and the Soviet Union were broken off in 1980 because of the USSR's invasion of Afghanistan in 1979.
- ☑ The Senate refused to sign SALT 2, despite Carter and Brezhnev having signed it in 1979.
- ☑ The arms race escalated when the USA restarted building nuclear and conventional weapons. The USSR reacted by developing a new medium-range missile, the SS20.

> **DID YOU KNOW?**
>
> The USA failed to ratify SALT 2 after the USSR invaded Afghanistan.
>
> However, détente was already under threat by other world events such as the USSR's support of communist groups in South America.

SOVIET INVASION OF AFGHANISTAN, 1979
The Afghanistan War has been called the USSR's Vietnam; a war it could not win and fought at very high cost.

What was the Afghan war?
The Soviet-Afghan War was fought between a group of Afghan rebels called the Mujahideen, supported by the USA, and the Soviet-supported Afghan government.

When was the Soviet Afghan War?
The Soviet-Afghan War lasted more than nine years, from December 1979 to February 1989.

Why was the USA concerned about the Afghan war?
The USA became involved because President Carter was concerned about 2 main issues:
- ☑ Increased Soviet control of the Middle East.
- ☑ The possibility of the USSR gaining control of Gulf oil fields.

Why did the Soviet Union start a war with Afghanistan?
There were 5 key reasons the USSR invaded Afghanistan:
- ☑ Afghanistan bordered the Soviet Union. For Brezhnev, this meant it fell within the Soviet sphere of influence.

- In April 1978, the Kabul Revolution occurred in Afghanistan. Taraki, a communist, became the new prime minister, an ally of the USSR, and brought in communist reforms.
- By spring 1979, a civil war broke out in Afghanistan between the communist government and the mujahideen (Islamic fighters).
- In October 1979, Taraki was assassinated in the civil war and replaced by Hafizullah Amin.
- After the Afghan government asked the USSR for help, the USSR invaded on 25th December, 1979.

 What were the consequences of the Soviet-Afghan war?

There were 6 main consequences of the Afghan war:

- The USSR's invasion of Afghanistan led to the Carter Doctrine (p.60). President Carter stated the USA would not allow the USSR to expand its influence in the Middle East.
- It ended détente (p.54) between the USA and the USSR. SALT 2 (p.58) was not ratified.
- It led to the boycott of the Moscow Olympic Games in 1980 by the USA and 61 other countries. The USSR retaliated by boycotting the Los Angeles Olympic Games in 1984.
- It led to American economic sanctions on the USSR. The USA would not sell grain or technology to the Soviets.
- This helped Ronald Reagan (p.61) win the 1980 election. His tough attitude to the Soviet Union was attractive to the American people.
- The war in Afghanistan had a devastating economic effect on the USSR. There were many casualties on both sides, which led to increased internal opposition to the Soviet leadership.

> **DID YOU KNOW?**
>
> President Gorbachev referred to the Soviet-Afghan War as a 'bleeding wound' in 1986.

CARTER DOCTRINE, 1980

President Carter issued the Carter Doctrine to prevent the expansion of Soviet influence in the Middle East.

What was the Carter doctrine?

The Carter Doctrine stated the USA was prepared to use military force should the USSR try to control the Persian Gulf and threaten America's interests there. It was an extension of the Truman Doctrine (p.30) to the Middle East.

When was the Carter Doctrine created?

The Carter Doctrine was created on 23rd January, 1980.

Who created the Carter Doctrine?

President Jimmy Carter created the Carter Doctrine.

 What were the consequences of the Carter Doctrine?

There were 4 main consequences of the Carter Doctrine.

- Economic sanctions were imposed on the USSR, which meant American companies could not sell computers and oil drilling technology to the Soviets.
- The USA refused to export grain to or import oil from the USSR.

- All countries neighbouring Afghanistan were promised military aid by the USA.
- This marked a new period of confrontation between the Cold War *(p.16)* superpowers. It was called the Second Cold War.

DID YOU KNOW?

President Carter addressed the American nation on the USSR's invasion of Afghanistan.

He stated, 'History teaches perhaps very few clear lessons. But surely one such lesson learned ... is that aggression unopposed becomes a contagious disease.'

PRESIDENT RONALD REAGAN, 1981

Ronald Reagan's policies increased tensions between the United States and the USSR.

Who was Ronald Reagan?

Ronald Reagan was the 40th president of the United States. He entered the White House with a desire to win the Cold War *(p.16)*.

When was Ronald Reagan the President of the USA?

Reagan served as the 40th president of the United States from 1981 to 1989.

What happened to the arms race under Ronald Reagan?

Reagan restarted the arms race with the USSR in 5 key ways:

- He increased investment in the armed forces.
- New weapons such as stealth bombers were developed.
- He did not believe in mutually assured destruction (that using nuclear weapons would destroy both the USA and the USSR).
- He believed you could have a limited nuclear war through nuclear utilisation target selection (NUTs) by targeting the USSR's weapons so they could not retaliate.
- He rejected Truman's Doctrine of containment. He did not want to accept the existence of communists in any part of the world, so he increased the arms race.

What was Ronald Reagan's 'Evil Empire' speech?

Reagan called the USSR the 'Evil Empire' in a speech in 1983. He implied the Cold War *(p.16)* was a war between good and evil and, as the USA was a religious nation, it should win the Cold War.

What was the Second Cold War during Ronald Reagan's presidency?

The Second Cold War *(p.16)* refers to the time after the end of détente *(p.54)*. It was a period of increased tension and the arms race restarted between the USA and the USSR.

What was President Reagan's 'Zero Option'?

In November 1981, Reagan offered to cancel the deployment of intermediate-range missiles in Europe if the USSR dismantled theirs. Brezhnev rejected Zero Option.

Why did President Reagan support Solidarity in Poland?
Reagan supported Solidarity, a Polish independent, non-communist trade union, for 2 main reasons:
- [x] It opposed the Polish communist government.
- [x] He hoped it would help end communism in Poland.

> **DID YOU KNOW?**
> Ronald Reagan had been an actor in Hollywood and the Governor of California.

STRATEGIC DEFENSE INITIATIVE (SDI), 1983
The SDI programme was an attempt to put lasers in space.

What was the Strategic Defence Initiative (SDI) or 'Star Wars'?
The Strategic Defense Initiative (SDI) was an American policy that aimed to develop a system of satellites in space to protect the USA from missile attacks by the USSR.

When was the Strategic Defense Initiative (SDI), or Star Wars, first initiated?
The Strategic Defense Initiative (SDI) was announced on 23rd March, 1983.

Who initiated the Strategic Defense Initiative (SDI)?
President Ronald Reagan *(p.61)* created the SDI programme.

What was the nickname of the Strategic Defense Initiative (SDI)?
The Strategic Defense Initiative (SDI) was nicknamed 'Star Wars'.

What was the importance of the Strategic Defense Initiative?
There were 4 main reasons SDI was important:
- [x] SDI broke the terms of the 1967 Outer Space Treaty *(p.49)* because it would put weapons in space.
- [x] It put enormous pressure on the USSR to increase investment in the arms race, something it could not afford.
- [x] It therefore encouraged Gorbachev to bring in reforms when he became leader of the USSR in 1985.
- [x] It put pressure on the USSR to negotiate with the USA on arms limitations/reductions to ease the economic pressure it was under.

> **DID YOU KNOW?**
> The Strategic Defense Initiative was nicknamed 'Star Wars', after the movie.

MIKHAIL GORBACHEV, 1985-1991
'I like Mr Gorbachev. We can do business together.' - British prime minister Margaret Thatcher, 1984

Who was Mikhail Gorbachev?
Mikhail Gorbachev was a member of the Communist Party in the USSR. He was appointed general secretary of the Soviet Union in 1985, a post he held until its collapse in 1991.

When was Mikhail Gorbachev in power?
Gorbachev was leader from 1985 to 1991, when the Soviet Union collapsed.

What did Mikhail Gorbachev realise when he came to power?
Gorbachev realised 4 key things about the USSR:
- People were unhappy about, and distrustful of, the Soviet government.
- The USSR's economy was stagnating with barely any industrial growth.
- People's standard of living was low and this was causing discontent and unrest.
- The Soviet Union was suffering because of the huge investment in weapons.

What were Mikhail Gorbachev's beliefs when he first came to power?
When Gorbachev came to power in 1985, he believed economic and political reform would solve the Soviet Union's problems and save communism. This led to the policies of 'perestroika' *(p.64)* and 'glasnost' *(p.64)*.

What were Mikhail Gorbachev's policies?
Gorbachev introduced 4 key new policies or reforms:
- Perestroika *(p.64)*, which means 'restructuring' and was the term used by Gorbachev to refer to his economic reforms.
- Glasnost *(p.64)*, which means 'openness'.
- He dropped the Brezhnev Doctrine *(p.53)* which had controlled eastern Europe since 1968.
- He reduced arms spending and withdrew from Afghanistan.

What changes were there in eastern Europe under Mikhail Gorbachev's rule?
There were 4 major changes to the countries of the Eastern Bloc under Gorbachev.
- Gorbachev allowed Eastern bloc countries to have more of a say in how their governments were run.
- The Brezhnev Doctrine *(p.53)* officially ended in December 1988 and was replaced by the 'Sinatra Doctrine'. Each country would be allowed to find its own path to socialism.
- Gorbachev focused on allowing openness in the Eastern Bloc, thinking this would lead to higher living standards.
- The USSR would no longer favour eastern Europe in trade, so they would buy goods from any country. It reduced the USSR's control over, and connection to, eastern Europe.

DID YOU KNOW?

Gorbachev was awarded the Nobel Peace Prize in 1990 for helping to end the Cold War.

PERESTROIKA

'A real revolution of the consciousness is under way without which it is impossible to create a new life'. Gorbachev on Perestroika, 1988

What was perestroika?
Perestroika is the Russian word for economic restructuring. It meant the communist economic system would be reformed to include some capitalist elements, such as small, privately owned businesses.

When was perestroika?
Perestroika lasted from 1985 until 1991.

Who used the term perestroika?
Mikhail Gorbachev introduced perestroika.

Why was perestroika important?
Perestroika was important in 3 main ways because:
- ☑ It failed to solve the USSR's economic problems and instead made them worse.
- ☑ Some people believe it was a significant factor in triggering the revolutions of 1989 across eastern Europe.
- ☑ It contributed to the collapse of the Soviet Union, which marked the end of the Cold War *(p.16)*.

DID YOU KNOW?

The economic restructuring that was brought in actually caused the USSR's economic situation to deteriorate even more.

GLASNOST

'Without glasnost there is not, and there cannot be, democratism, the political creativity of the masses and their participation in management'. Gorbachev, 1988

What was glasnost?
Glasnost generally means openness in Russian. It was a Soviet policy to allow open discussion of political and social issues with the aim of saving and improving communism.

When was glasnost introduced?
In 1986, Mikhail Gorbachev and his advisers adopted 'glasnost' as a political policy.

Who introduced glasnost?
In 1985, Mikhail Gorbachev came to power. The two reforms most commonly associated with him are glasnost and perestroika *(p.64)*.

What's the importance of glasnost?
Glasnost was important in 4 main ways:

- It led to a decrease in media censorship.
- It resulted in writers and journalists exposing government corruption and the depths of poverty in the USSR.
- This in turn led to increased criticism of the communist government and encouraged democratisation.
- It helped contribute to the collapse of the USSR and the end of the Cold War (p.16).

> **DID YOU KNOW?**
> Under Gorbachev, Russia's first McDonald's opened in Moscow in 1990.

REAGAN AND GORBACHEV'S RELATIONSHIP
The personal relationship that developed between Reagan and Gorbachev was important in helping to improve relations between the two countries.

What was the relationship between Reagan and Gorbachev, and their political positions?
Reagan and Gorbachev first met at a summit in Geneva. They got on well and arranged further meetings. Gorbachev was popular, even in western Europe and the United States.

When did Gorbachev and Reagan first meet?
Reagan and Gorbachev first met in 1985 in Geneva.

Which other political leader supported the Reagan-Gorbachev relationship?
Margaret Thatcher, the British Prime Minister, supported Reagan and was willing to work with Gorbachev too.

What was the importance of the Reagan-Gorbachev relationship?
Their relationship led to more cooperation and less tension between the USSR and the USA. The Cold War (p.16) began to fizzle out.

> **DID YOU KNOW?**
> **The relationship did not start well.**
> Reagan called the USSR the 'evil empire' in 1983 and Gorbachev called Reagan a 'caveman'.

GENEVA SUMMIT, 1985
Geneva was the first meeting between Reagan and Gorbachev.

What was discussed at the Geneva Summit?
Reagan and Gorbachev (p.65) met for the first time at the Geneva Summit, where they discussed limiting the arms race and SDI (p.62).

When was the Geneva Summit?
It took place in November 1985.

What was agreed at the Geneva Summit?
The Geneva Accord was agreed, which said Gorbachev and Reagan would:
- ☑ Speed up arms talks.
- ☑ Work towards getting rid of chemical weapons.
- ☑ Make a new commitment to human rights.

What disagreements were there at the Geneva Summit?
Reagan and Gorbachev *(p.65)* did not come to any official agreement over arms limitations because Reagan would not drop SDI *(p.62)*.

Why was the Geneva Summit between Reagan and Gorbachev important?
The Geneva Summit was important in 3 main ways because:
- ☑ Reagan and Gorbachev *(p.65)* developed a good working relationship and a strong personal relationship.
- ☑ Both wanted to improve relations between their countries.
- ☑ It led to the next summit meeting in Reykjavik in 1986.

> **DID YOU KNOW?**
>
> **In November 1985, President Ronald Reagan commented about meeting Mikhail Gorbachev for the first time.**
>
> Reagan said, 'There was a warmth in his face and style, not the coldness bordering on hatred I'd seen in most other senior Soviet leaders I'd met until then.'

REYKJAVIK SUMMIT, 1986
The summit at Reykjavik was different because Gorbachev proposed the elimination of all nuclear weapons.

What were the discussions at Reykjavik?
At the Reykjavik Summit, Reagan and Gorbachev *(p.65)* discussed arms reduction and limitations. Gorbachev proposed phasing out nuclear weapons if the USA gave up its SDI *(p.62)* programme.

When was the Reykjavik Summit?
It took place in Iceland on 11th October, 1986.

Why was the Reykjavik summit important?
The Reykjavik summit meeting was important because the relationship between Gorbachev and Reagan continued to improve, with both willing to discuss arms limitations.

What disagreements were there at the Reykjavik Summit?

Reagan refused to end the SDI *(p.62)* programme and, as a result, no formal agreement was reached.

> **DID YOU KNOW?**
>
> Gorbachev was very serious about his proposal to eliminate nuclear weapons.
>
> The economic situation in the USSR was so dire he was desperate to cut military spending.

WASHINGTON SUMMIT, 1987

The Washington Summit was the most significant of the three meetings because of the outcomes.

What were the discussions at Washington?

At the Washington Summit, Reagan and Gorbachev *(p.65)* discussed arms reductions and limitations. Gorbachev finally agreed to disarmament even though Reagan would not abandon SDI *(p.62)*.

When was the Washington Summit?

It took place in December, 1987.

Why were the Washington discussions between Reagan and Gorbachev important?

The Washington summit meeting was very important because it resulted in the signing of the Intermediate-Range Nuclear Force (INF) Treaty *(p.67)*.

> **DID YOU KNOW?**
>
> The Washington Summit was the first time a leader of the Soviet Union had visited the USA since 1973.

INTERMEDIATE-RANGE NUCLEAR FORCE (INF) TREATY, 1987

The INF Treaty was the first time both sides in the Cold War agreed to dismantle existing nuclear weapons.

What was the INF treaty?

The Intermediate-Range Nuclear Forces Treaty was an arms control treaty between the USA and the Soviet Union.

When was the INF treaty signed?

It was signed in Washington DC on 8th December, 1987.

Who signed the INF treaty?
President Reagan and Soviet General Secretary Gorbachev signed the INF treaty.

What was the INF treaty about?
The Intermediate-Range Nuclear Forces (INF) Treaty of 1987 had 2 main terms:
- ✓ The USA and the USSR would destroy their ground-launched missiles with a range of 500 to 5,500 km.
- ✓ The treaty primarily affected Europe, where most of these missiles were located.

Why was the INF treaty important?
The INF Treaty was important because it was the first time during the Cold War *(p.16)* that nuclear weapons would actually be destroyed, reducing the total number.

DID YOU KNOW?
By June 1991, 2692 missiles had been dismantled as a result of the INF Treaty.

MOSCOW SUMMIT, 1988
During the Moscow Summit, Reagan said the Cold War was over.

What was discussed at Moscow?
At the Moscow Summit, Reagan and Gorbachev *(p.65)* had further discussions about limiting nuclear arms and conventional arms. They also discussed some details of the Intermediate-Range Nuclear Forces (INF) Treaty *(p.67)*.

When was the Moscow Summit?
Reagan and Gorbachev *(p.65)* met in Moscow in May 1988.

Why were the Moscow discussions between Reagan and Gorbachev important?
The Moscow Summit was important because it opened the way to future agreements that took place when George Bush became President of the USA.

What disagreements were there at the Moscow Summit?
No agreement was reached on limitations of nuclear or conventional arms.

DID YOU KNOW?
During his visit to Moscow, Reagan gave a speech to students at the Moscow State University and toured Red Square.

MALTA SUMMIT, 1988

'We are at the beginning of a long road to a lasting, peaceful era.' - Mikhail Gorbachev at the Malta Summit

What was discussed at Malta?
President George Bush and Gorbachev met in Malta to continue discussions on arms limitations.

When were the Malta discussions?
Bush and Gorbachev met in Malta in May 1988.

Why were the Malta discussions between Bush and Gorbachev important?
Both the USA and the USSR saw the summit in Malta as the beginning of the end of the Cold War *(p.16)*. Their discussions at Malta resulted in the 1990 Conventional Armed Forces in Europe (CFE *(p.69)*) agreement and START *(p.70)* I in 1991.

> **DID YOU KNOW?**
>
> **Gorbachev met with President George Bush Senior for the first time at the Malta Conference.**
>
> At the end of the conference, the two leaders held a joint press conference on board the Maxim Gorky, a Soviet cruise ship.

TREATY ON CONVENTIONAL ARMED FORCES IN EUROPE, 1990

The CFE Treaty helped to reduce tension in Europe.

What was the Treaty on Conventional Armed Forces in Europe?
The Treaty on Conventional Armed Forces in Europe limited the non-nuclear or conventional forces of NATO *(p.36)* and the Warsaw Pact *(p.37)*. The treaty applied to Europe.

When was the Treaty on Conventional Armed Forces signed?
The CFE treaty was signed on 19th November, 1990.

Who signed the Treaty on Conventional Armed Forces?
President Bush and Soviet General Secretary Gorbachev signed the CFE Treaty.

Why was the Treaty on Conventional Armed Forces important?
The CFE Treaty was important because it helped reduce tension in Europe and made war less likely.

> **DID YOU KNOW?**
>
> In 2007, President Putin withdrew Russia from the CFE Treaty.

STRATEGIC ARMS REDUCTION TREATY (START I) 1991

The START treaty continued the process of nuclear weapons reduction.

What was the Strategic Arms Reduction Treaty (START I) 1991?
START, or the Strategic Arms Reduction Treaty, set limits to the number of nuclear weapons the USSR and the USA could hold and reduced most types of nuclear weapons by one third.

When was the Strategic Arms Reduction Treaty signed?
It was signed on 31st July, 1991.

Who signed the Strategic Arms Reduction Treaty?
President Bush and Soviet General Secretary Gorbachev signed START I.

Why was the Strategic Arms Reduction Treaty important?
START was important because both sides would subsequently destroy their nuclear weapons. They would also continue to reduce the number of nuclear weapons they had.

DID YOU KNOW?

President Bush and President Mikhail Gorbachev signed the START agreement with pens made from dismantled missiles.

THE COLLAPSE OF SOVIET CONTROL OF EASTERN EUROPE, 1989-1990

Replacing the Brezhnev Doctrine with the Sinatra Doctrine paved the way for the end of USSR control over eastern Europe.

What happened to the USSR's control over eastern Europe?
The USSR lost control of its satellite states in eastern Europe when the people of each country rose in protest against their communist governments and the USSR did not stop them.

When did the USSR lose control of its satellite states in eastern Europe?
The USSR lost control of eastern Europe between June 1989 and December 1990.

Why did the USSR lose control of its satellite states?
There were 8 key reasons:
- ✓ The USSR was struggling economically and could not afford to keep control.
- ✓ Reagan increased economic pressure by increasing military spending, forcing the USSR out of the arms race.
- ✓ Economic and social problems, plus government corruption, caused a low standard of living which weakened support for communism.
- ✓ Gorbachev encouraged eastern Europe to implement perestroika *(p.64)*.
- ✓ Gorbachev had brought in political reforms under glasnost *(p.64)* which encouraged eastern Europe to reform.

- Gorbachev ended the Brezhnev Doctrine *(p.53)* and stated eastern Europe no longer had to be afraid the USSR would intervene. He also reduced military spending.
- The USSR's new approach was called the Sinatra Doctrine; eastern Europe was free to choose how it would be governed.
- Successful protest movements, such as Solidarity in Poland.

 What happened in each country when USSR control was lost over eastern Europe?

There was a series of 7 main uprisings across eastern Europe:

- Hungary took down the border fence with Austria in May 1989 and allowed free elections in December.
- After massive demonstrations in Poland, independent trade union Solidarity was legalised and won the elections in June 1989.
- In September 1989, thousands of East Germans fled to Austria through Hungary. In November 1989, the border between East and West Berlin was opened and people started to pull down the Berlin Wall *(p 43)*.
- In November 1989, a non-violent 'Velvet Revolution' occurred in Czechoslovakia that overthrew the communist government.
- Romania saw massive demonstrations that became violent when the communist government tried to crush them. The communist leader, Nicolae Ceausescu, was arrested, put on trial and executed in December 1989.
- In December 1989, the communist leader in Bulgaria resigned and free elections were held in 1990.
- In December 1990, Slovenians voted in a referendum to become independent, a decision which resulted in the break up of Yugoslavia.

 What were the results of the loss of USSR control over eastern Europe?

There were 4 key results:

- All the satellite states held free elections and the communists lost their power.
- The reunification of Germany took place in 1990.
- The Warsaw Pact *(p.37)* was no longer relevant. Military cooperation ended and in July 1991 the pact was officially dissolved.
- Inside the USSR, the loss of eastern Europe angered leading Communist Party officials. This led to an attempt to remove Gorbachev from power by the Gang of 8.

> **DID YOU KNOW?**
>
> **Abandoning the Brezhnev Doctrine was a significant shift in the USSR's relationship with eastern Europe.**
>
> Gorbachev informed the leaders of the eastern European countries about the change at the funeral of Konstantin Chernenko, the previous leader of the USSR.

FALL OF THE BERLIN WALL, 1989

The fall of the Berlin Wall was momentous.

 What was the fall of the Berlin Wall?

Throughout the summer of 1989, demand for change grew in many East German cities. With the protests escalating, the Berlin Wall *(p.43)* was eventually brought down. This was a symbolic marker of communist collapse.

When did the Berlin Wall fall?
The Berlin Wall *(p.43)* fell on 9th November, 1989.

What were the consequences of the fall of the Berlin Wall?
There were 5 main consequences of the fall of the Berlin wall.
- Soviet troops were withdrawn from East Germany.
- It encouraged people in other eastern European countries to rise up against communist rule.
- Soviet troops then withdrew from many other eastern European countries from 1990 onwards.
- US, French and British troops were still posted in West Germany.
- It eventually led to the reunification of East and West Germany into one country in November 1990.

Why was the fall of the Berlin Wall important?
The fall of the wall was the main symbol of communist collapse in eastern Europe and led to the reunification of Germany.

> **DID YOU KNOW?**
>
> **Berliners took sledge hammers and even drills to the wall to chip it away piece by piece.**
>
> It took about two years to remove the Berlin Wall. Some sections have been left, such as the East Side Gallery, which has been painted.

GORBACHEV'S FALL FROM POWER
Gorbachev's reforms inadvertently led to his own downfall.

What was Gorbachev's fall from power?
During 1990 and 1991 Gorbachev faced massive domestic problems which led to his resignation as leader of the USSR.

When did Gorbachev fall from power?
Gorbachev struggled throughout 1991, eventually resigning on 25th December that year.

Why did Gorbachev fall from power?
There were 5 main reasons Gorbachev fell from power:
- His reforms of 'perestroika *(p.64)*' and 'glasnost *(p.64)*' had not solved the USSR's economic and political problems.
- The Soviet economy was in a terrible state, with food rationing and long queues in the shops for goods.
- Glasnost *(p.64)* allowed people to criticise the government and people started to criticise Gorbachev's policies.
- Many Communist Party leaders and ordinary people were angry when the USSR lost control of eastern Europe. They blamed Gorbachev for weakening the Soviet Union.
- Political opposition to Gorbachev grew when Latvia, Estonia and Lithuania declared their independence from the USSR in 1990.

How did Gorbachev fall from power?

There were 5 key events during Gorbachev's fall from power:

- ☑ On 19th August 1990, 8 senior members of the Communist Party and government organised a coup against Gorbachev and placed him under house arrest.
- ☑ The new government declared a state of emergency and ended Gorbachev's policies of 'glasnost *(p.64)*' and 'perestroika *(p.64)*'.
- ☑ People reacted by demonstrating against the new government, led by Boris Yeltsin, a senior ex-member of the Communist Party, who used the coup to undermine Gorbachev.
- ☑ On 21st August, Gorbachev returned to Moscow. He tried to bring in a new constitution and New Union Treaty to keep the USSR alive.
- ☑ Boris Yeltsin persuaded 12 of the 15 leaders of the other Soviet republics to create the Commonwealth of Independent States (CIS), using Gorbachev's weakened position against him.

What were the results of Gorbachev's fall from power?

There were 2 main results:

- ☑ When 12 of the 15 Soviet republics signed the Commonwealth of Independent States agreement it meant the USSR no longer existed as a country.
- ☑ Gorbachev resigned as leader of the USSR on 25th December, 1991.

> **DID YOU KNOW?**
> 'Fate had it that when I found myself at the head of the state it was already clear all was not well in the country,' Gorbachev said in his resignation speech.

THE COLLAPSE OF THE USSR, 1990-91
With the end of the USSR came the end of the Cold War.

How did the Soviet Union collapse?

There were 6 key events which led to the collapse of the USSR:

- ☑ Gorbachev attempted to reform the USSR to save communism.
- ☑ The USSR lost control of eastern Europe between 1989 and 1990 because of Gorbachev's reforms.
- ☑ There was an attempted coup against Gorbachev by the Gang of 8 in August 1991.
- ☑ Gorbachev's attempt to introduce a new constitution and a New Union Treaty to save the USSR was rejected.
- ☑ When the 12 Soviet republics signed the Commonwealth of Independent States agreement it meant the USSR no longer existed as a country.
- ☑ In December 1991, Gorbachev dissolved the Soviet Union in his final act as president.

> **DID YOU KNOW?**
> The flag of the USSR was lowered for the final time on the night of 25th December, 1991.

HAFIZULLAH AMIN
President Hafizullah Amin ruled Afghanistan for five months.

Who was Hafizullah Amin?
Hafizullah Amin overthrew the Taraki government in Afghanistan in 1979.

Who invaded while Amin was leader?
Amin was initially supported by Moscow. However, the Soviets became suspicious and believed he was a CIA spy, leading them to invade Afghanistan.

> **DID YOU KNOW?**
> Hafizullah Amin was assassinated, first by being poisoned and then shot on 27th December, 1979.

PRIME MINISTER ATTLEE
Clement Attlee was the British Prime Minister from 1945 to 1951.

Who was Clement Attlee?
Clement Attlee was a Labour politician who served as prime minister of the United Kingdom from 1945 to 1951.

What were Clement Attlee's beliefs?
Attlee had left-wing beliefs and his government is most famous for creating the NHS. Attlee supported the Marshall Plan *(p.31)* and promoted a NATO *(p.36)* military alliance against the USSR and its satellite states.

What conferences did Clement Attlee attend?
Attlee attended the Potsdam Conference *(p.21)* in July 1945, to discuss Nazi Germany and how to end the war.

> **DID YOU KNOW?**
> Attlee trained as a lawyer, fought in the First World War and was the founding father of the NHS.

FULGENCIO BATISTA
Fulgencio Batista was nicknamed 'El Hombre', or ' the man'.

Who was Batista?
Fulgencio Batista was the American-backed dictator of Cuba from 1952 to 1959, until he was overthrown by Fidel Castro in the Cuban Revolution *(p.44)*.

> **DID YOU KNOW?**
>
> After the Cuban Revolution, Batista lived in exile in various places, including Spain and Portugal.

LEONID BREZHNEV

Leonid Brezhnev was the fourth leader of the USSR.

 Who was Leonid Brezhnev?

Leonid Brezhnev was the fifth leader of the Soviet Union from 1964 until his death in 1982.

 What was the doctrine Brezhnev used?

The Brezhnev Doctrine *(p.53)* was established in 1968. This stated that the actions of an individual communist country affected all communist countries, therefore others must take action to ensure the survival of the regime.

 What was Brezhnev's reaction to Reagan's Zero Option proposal?

Brezhnev rejected President Reagan's Zero Option proposal in November 1981, in which Reagan offered to cancel the deployment of intermediate-range missiles in Europe if the USSR dismantled theirs.

> **DID YOU KNOW?**
>
> Brezhnev's rule of the USSR is marked by stagnation and corruption.

PRESIDENT JIMMY CARTER

President Carter was a member of the Democratic Party.

 Who was President Carter?

Jimmy Carter was the 39th President of the United States from 1977 to 1981.

 What were President Carter's thoughts on the USSR?

Carter was shocked by the Soviet invasion of Afghanistan and released a statement known as the Carter Doctrine *(p.60)*. This stated he would not allow the USSR to control the Middle East.

> **DID YOU KNOW?**
>
> President Carter was awarded a Nobel Peace Prize in 2002 for 'his decades of untiring effort to find peaceful solutions to international conflicts, to advance democracy and human rights, and to promote economic and social development'.

PRIME MINISTER CHURCHILL
Prime Minister Churchill led Britain during the Second World War.

Who was Winston Churchill?
Sir Winston Churchill was Prime Minister of the United Kingdom from 1940 to 1945, and again from 1951 to 1955.

What were Churchill's beliefs?
Churchill was a conservative with traditional values. He strongly valued democracy, was in favour of empire, and was incredibly suspicious of Stalin.

What conferences did Churchill attend?
Churchill attended the Tehran and Yalta conferences to discuss Nazi Germany and how to end the war.

What was Churchill's 'Iron Curtain' speech?
In March 1946, Churchill made a speech in the USA that criticised the USSR and called it a threat to world peace. Stalin thought this reflected America's beliefs. This speech is referred to as the 'Iron Curtain' speech *(p.29)*.

What was Churchill's views on the policy of appeasement?
Winston Churchill was an opponent of appeasement, describing it as 'an unmitigated disaster'. Churchill told Britain and France they would have to choose between war and dishonour, and that Hitler was not done expanding the Third Reich.

DID YOU KNOW?

Churchill lost the general election to Attlee in July 1945.
Churchill actually attended the Potsdam Conference but was replaced by Attlee as the new British Prime Minister.

ALEXANDER DUBČEK
'Socialism with a human face.' Alexander Dubček

Who was Dubček?
Alexander Dubček was a leader of Czechoslovakia. He had a good relationship with Soviet leader Leonid Brezhnev, supported the Warsaw Pact *(p.37)* and wanted to introduce reforms to improve people's lives.

When was Dubček in power?
Alexander Dubček was the leader of Czechoslovakia from January 1968 to August 1968.

What were Dubček reforms called?
Dubček introduced reforms known as the Prague Spring *(p.51)* to create 'socialism with a human face'.

What reforms did Dubček introduce?
There were 4 main reforms introduced by Dubček:
- He relaxed censorship.
- Other political parties were also permitted.
- The secret police had their powers reduced.
- Some capitalist elements were even allowed to create a form of "market socialism" economy.

What happened to Dubček afterwards?
The following happened to Dubček:
- Dubček was arrested and forced to visit Moscow.
- He was ordered to reverse all his reforms.
- In 1969, Dubček was replaced by Husak, who was a hardline communist Moscow could rely on.
- He was appointed Ambassador to Turkey until he was expelled from the party, and then he worked in forest administration.

> **DID YOU KNOW?**
>
> Dubček believed Lenin (the first leader of the Soviet Union) had been wrong about some things, and that allowing some elements of capitalism was necessary.

PRESIDENT EISENHOWER

There were key events in the Cold War when President Eisenhower was in power: the Korean War, the creation of the Warsaw Pact, Khrushchev's 'Secret Speech', and the U2 spy plane incident were among them.

Who was President Eisenhower?
Dwight D Eisenhower was the 34th President of the United States.

When was Eisenhower president?
Eisenhower was President of the United States from 1953 until 1961.

What was President Eisenhower's background?
President Eisenhower's background included the following:
- Eisenhower was a member of the US armed forces throughout the 1920s and 1930s.
- He was a general in the army during the Second World War and was in charge of the D-Day landings in 1944.
- He became the supreme commander of NATO *(p.36)* in December 1950.
- His war record helped him secure the presidency.

What were the key events of Eisenhower's presidency?
Some of the key events of Eisenhower's presidency included:
- In 1953 he helped negotiate an armistice that brought peace to Korea.

- ✅ He committed the USA to protecting South Vietnam from communism in 1953.
- ✅ He was in power during the Montgomery Bus Boycott, led by Rosa Parks, which lasted for twelve months between 1955 and 1956.
- ✅ In 1957 he signed the Civil Rights Act and set up a permanent Civil Rights Commission.

What were Eisenhower's beliefs about the Cold War?
Eisenhower was anti-communist and committed to the policy of containment. He articulated the concept of the 'Domino Theory'.

What uprising was Eisenhower involved in?
Eisenhower managed to increase tensions between the East and the West when he refused to send US troops to help the Hungarian Uprisings. This led to Eastern Bloc countries realising the West would not support them.

Did Eisenhower send a spy to the USSR?
In 1960, Khrushchev walked out of a meeting after Eisenhower refused to apologise for sending a U2 spy plane to spy on the Soviet Union.

What actions did Eisenhower take on civil rights?
Eisenhower took 3 key actions related to civil rights:

- ✅ He introduced the Civil Rights Act of 1957 that sought to ensure all African Americans could register to vote.
- ✅ Following the ruling in the case of Brown v Board of Education, Eisenhower did not want to use his powers to support the rapid desegregation of schools as he believed it should proceed slowly.
- ✅ He sent federal troops to Little Rock to protect the African American students and enforce integration.

> **DID YOU KNOW?**
>
> **President Eisenhower gave a speech called 'Chance for Peace' after Stalin died.**
>
> In that speech, he called on the USSR to work for peace.

MIKHAIL GORBACHEV
Mikhail Gorbachev was the last leader of the USSR.

Who was Mikhail Gorbachev?
Mikhail Gorbachev was a member of the Communist Party in the USSR. He was appointed general secretary of the Soviet Union in 1985, a post he held until its collapse in 1991.

When was Mikhail Gorbachev in power?
Gorbachev was leader from 1985 to 1991, when the Soviet Union collapsed.

What did Mikhail Gorbachev realise when he came to power?
Gorbachev realised 4 key things about the USSR:

- ✅ People were unhappy about, and distrustful of, the Soviet government.

- The USSR's economy was stagnating with barely any industrial growth.
- People's standard of living was low and this was causing discontent and unrest.
- The Soviet Union was suffering because of the huge investment in weapons.

What were Mikhail Gorbachev's beliefs when he first came to power?

When Gorbachev came to power in 1985, he believed economic and political reform would solve the Soviet Union's problems and save communism. This led to the policies of 'perestroika' (p.64) and 'glasnost' (p.64).

What were Mikhail Gorbachev's policies?

Gorbachev introduced 4 key new policies or reforms:

- Perestroika (p.64), which means 'restructuring' and was the term used by Gorbachev to refer to his economic reforms.
- Glasnost (p.64), which means 'openness'.
- He dropped the Brezhnev Doctrine (p.53) which had controlled eastern Europe since 1968.
- He reduced arms spending and withdrew from Afghanistan.

What changes were there in eastern Europe under Mikhail Gorbachev's rule?

There were 4 major changes to the countries of the Eastern Bloc under Gorbachev.

- Gorbachev allowed Eastern bloc countries to have more of a say in how their governments were run.
- The Brezhnev Doctrine (p.53) officially ended in December 1988 and was replaced by the 'Sinatra Doctrine'. Each country would be allowed to find its own path to socialism.
- Gorbachev focused on allowing openness in the Eastern Bloc, thinking this would lead to higher living standards.
- The USSR would no longer favour eastern Europe in trade, so they would buy goods from any country. It reduced the USSR's control over, and connection to, eastern Europe.

DID YOU KNOW?

In 1997, Gorbachev appeared in an advert for Pizza Hut with his granddaughter.

GEORGE KENNAN

George F Kennan was a historian and a diplomat.

Who was George Kennan?

George Kennan was an American diplomat and the US ambassador in Moscow.

What were Kennan's beliefs?

Kennan was a strong advocate of the US policy of containment and was suspicious of the Soviet Union.

What telegram did Kennan send?

In 1946, Kennan sent the 'Long Telegram (p.22)' to Truman. This reported hostile attitudes in Moscow towards the USA and said Stalin wanted to destroy capitalism.

> **DID YOU KNOW?**
>
> It was Kennan's telegram, named after him, which coined the phrase 'containment' - the heart of the Truman Doctrine.

PRESIDENT JOHN F KENNEDY

President Kennedy stated, 'I take pride in the words Ich bin ein Berliner' when he visited Berlin.

Who was President Kennedy?
John F Kennedy, commonly referred to as JFK, was the 35th President of the United States.

When was Kennedy president?
John F Kennedy was president between January 1961 and November 1963.

What was Kennedy's background?
Kennedy's background included the following:
- He came from an Irish-American family which was very wealthy and heavily involved in politics.
- He went to Harvard University and studied politics. He wrote his dissertation on Britain's policy of the appeasement of Adolf Hitler.
- He was in the US navy and served in the Second World War, where he was seriously injured when his boat was destroyed by the Japanese.

What were the key events of Kennedy's presidency?
The key events of Kennedy's presidency included the following:
- Kennedy created the Peace Corps in 1961.
- The Bay of Pigs Invasion in Cuba, in April 1961.
- In May 1961 he pledged America would put a man on the moon by the end of the decade.
- The Berlin Wall *(p.43)* was built in 1961.
- The Cuban Missile Crisis *(p.46)* took place in October 1962.
- He signed the Limited Nuclear Test Ban Treaty in August 1963.

What were Kennedy's beliefs about the Cold War?
Kennedy was anti-communist and, like his predecessors, was committed to containing communism. However, he was aware of the dangers of nuclear warfare after tensions were brought to the brink during the Cuban Missile Crisis *(p.46)*, and wanted to reduce the chances of nuclear war.

What was President Kennedy's role in the Bay of Pigs invasion?
Kennedy attempted to implement a counter-revolution in Cuba by sending in Cuban exiles. The aim was to make it look like the USA wasn't involved. However, the plan failed.

What was President Kennedy's involvement with the Cuban Missile Crisis?

In 1962, two U2 spy planes spotted what looked like missiles in Cuba. This led to a tense 13 days where Kennedy deliberated what to do. He decided to set up a naval blockade and managed to prevent nuclear war.

 What was President Kennedy's role in Vietnam?

President Kennedy continued to support South Vietnam with money, military advisers and commandos.

 How did President Kennedy die?

Kennedy was assassinated in November 1963 in Dallas, Texas.

 Why was President Kennedy in Dallas?

Kennedy was in Dallas because he needed to win support from the southern Democrats, nicknamed the Dixiecrats, for his Civil Rights bill.

> **DID YOU KNOW?**
>
> **The Kennedy family was rich and powerful.**
> JFK's brothers, Robert and Ted, both became famous senators.

NIKITA KHRUSHCHEV

Nikita Khrushchev was third leader of the USSR.

 Who was Khrushchev?

Nikita Khrushchev led the Soviet Union after Stalin's death up until 1964.

 What was Khrushchev's speech?

Khrushchev openly criticised Stalin in his 'Secret Speech' in 1956. Khrushchev began to de-Stalinise the Soviet Union and said he wanted a peaceful co-existence with the West. People hoped this would end the Cold War *(p.16)*.

 How did tensions increase under Khrushchev?

The Hungarian Uprising *(p.40)* managed to increase international tensions as countries in eastern Europe began to realise the USA would not help them.

> **DID YOU KNOW?**
>
> **Khrushchev was the son of a peasant from Ukraine.**
> He was not well-educated but rose through the ranks of the Communist Party. Despite his criticism of Stalin's brutality in his 'Secret Speech', he was involved in the Great Purges of the 1930s.

GEORGE MARSHALL

George C Marshall had a long military career and was partly responsible for the Normandy invasion of 1944.

Who was Marshall?
George C Marshall was a general in the American army and statesman. He served as Secretary of State and Secretary of Defense under President Truman.

What plan did George Marshall come up with?
The Marshall Plan *(p.31)* aimed to provide economic aid to war-torn countries in Europe. The purpose of this was keep them tied to the USA instead of falling to communism.

> **DID YOU KNOW?**
>
> George C Marshall was awarded the Nobel Peace Prize in 1953 for creating the Marshall Plan.

IMRE NAGY

Imre Nagy was a life-long member of the Communist Party.

Who was Imre Nagy?
Imre Nagy was a Hungarian communist politician who served as Prime Minister from 1953 to 1955 and again during the Hungarian Uprising *(p.40)* in 1956.

What uprising was Nagy involved in?
Nagy introduced reforms that Khrushchev accepted. However, Nagy then announced that Hungary was leaving the Warsaw Pact *(p.37)*, so Khrushchev sent in the Red Army.

How did Nagy die?
As a result of the Hungarian Uprising *(p.40)*, Nagy was executed.

> **DID YOU KNOW?**
>
> Nagy was executed by hanging in 1958.

NIKOLAI NOVIKOV

Nikolai Novikov's telegram greatly influenced Stalin's attitudes towards the USA.

Who was Nikolai Novikov?
Nikolai Novikov was a Soviet diplomat and the USSR's ambassador in Washington.

What was Novikov's telegram?
Stalin received a telegram from Novikov which reported that America wanted to dominate the world and was preparing for war with the USSR.

> **DID YOU KNOW?**
> Nikolai Novikov was stationed in America from April 1946 to October 1947 as the Soviet Ambassador to the USA.

ANTONIN NOVOTNÝ

Antonin Novotný was a hard-line Stalinist.

Who was Novotný?
Antonin Novotný was the communist Prime Minister of Czechoslovakia from 1957 to 1968.

What important events occurred while Novotný was leader?
Novotný was leader when the Prague Spring *(p.51)* began, where people tried to reform the communist system in Czechoslovakia to create 'socialism with a human face'.

> **DID YOU KNOW?**
> Novotný was allowed to rejoin the Central Committee of the Czechoslovakian Communist Party after the Prague Spring but he never regained his power.

PRESIDENT ROOSEVELT

President Roosevelt played a key role in two of the three wartime meetings of the Grand Alliance.

What were President Roosevelt's beliefs during the Second World War?
President Roosevelt strongly believed in democracy. However, he formed an alliance with the USSR to protect the USA against Japan. He believed Stalin could be 'managed' and remain a post-war ally.

What conferences did Roosevelt attend at the end of the Second World War to discuss his ideas?
President Roosevelt attended the Tehran and Yalta conferences, which discussed Nazi Germany and how to end the war.

> **DID YOU KNOW?**
> President Roosevelt was awarded the Nobel Peace Prize in 1906 for his role in negotiating the Treaty of Portsmouth that ended the Russo-Japanese War.

NUR MUHAMMAD TARAKI

Nur Muhammad Taraki was the President of Afghanistan from 1978 to 1979.

Who was Taraki?

Nur Muhammad Taraki was a communist statesman in Afghanistan during the Cold War *(p.16)* and served as the country's president from 1978 to 1979.

What war was Taraki involved in?

Muslim leaders across Afghanistan didn't like the new communist leader. They started a civil war against the communists in spring 1979.

When did Taraki die?

Members of the communist government were fighting among themselves and, in October 1979, Amin supporters assassinated Taraki. Amin then claimed the presidency.

> **DID YOU KNOW?**
> Nur Muhammad Taraki died in the fighting when Amin staged a coup in 1979.

PRESIDENT HARRY TRUMAN

President Truman stated, 'I believe that it must be the policy of the United States to support free peoples who are resisting attempted subjugation by armed minorities or by outside pressures.'

Who was President Truman?

Harry S Truman was the 33rd President of the United States, holding office from 1945 to 1953.

What was an overview of Truman's time as president?

Truman's time as president included the following events:

- ✓ He took over from Franklin D Roosevelt during the Second World War.
- ✓ He oversaw huge challenges both domestically and internationally as America transitioned from fighting the Second World War in 1945 to the onset of the Cold War *(p.16)* between 1947 and 1949.
- ✓ His policy of the Truman Doctrine *(p.30)* and the policy of the containment became the cornerstone of American foreign policy for decades.
- ✓ In the years after his presidency he faced huge criticism as the president who 'lost China to communism'.

- ✓ He is now considered by historians to be one of America's greatest presidents.

What was President Truman's attitude towards communism?
Truman objected to the USSR's control over the countries of eastern Europe. He believed the USSR was determined to expand, so he sought to contain the spread of communism during his time in office.

What conferences did Truman attend?
Truman attended the Potsdam Conference *(p.21)* in July 1945 to discuss Nazi Germany and how to end the war.

What was Truman's involvement in the Cold War?
The Truman Doctrine *(p.30)*, in 1947, highlighted America's new stance on communism, and signalled the beginning of the US policy of containment.

DID YOU KNOW?

Harry S Truman's middle name was, literally, 'S'.
It was included to honour his grandfathers, who both had 'S' in their names.

GLOSSARY

A

Abdicate - to give up a position of power or a responsibility.

Abolish, Abolished - to stop something, or get rid of it.

Aggression - angry, hostile or violent behaviour displayed without provocation.

Agricultural - relating to agriculture.

Alliance - a union between groups or countries that benefits each member.

Allies - parties working together for a common objective, such as countries involved in a war. In both world wars, 'Allies' refers to those countries on the side of Great Britain.

Ambassador - someone, often a diplomat, who represents their state, country or organisation in a different setting or place.

Armistice - an agreement between two or more opposing sides in a war to stop fighting.

Assassinate - to murder someone, usually an important figure, often for religious or political reasons.

B

Blockade - a way of blocking or sealing an area to prevent goods, supplies or people from entering or leaving. It often refers to blocking transport routes.

Boycott - a way of protesting or bringing about change by refusing to buy something or use services.

Brinkmanship - pushing a disagreement to its limits in the hope the other side backs down, especially pertaining to war.

Buffer - a protective barrier.

Buffer zone - a neutral area of land to separate hostile forces or nations and provide protection. In the Cold War, Eastern Europe was the buffer zone between Western Europe and the USSR.

C

Cabinet - politically, the group of senior ministers responsible for controlling government policy.

Capitalism - the idea of goods and services being exchanged for money, private ownership of property and businesses, and acceptance of a hierarchical society.

Casualties - people who have been injured or killed, such as during a war, accident or catastrophe.

Censorship - the control of information in the media by a government, whereby information considered obscene or unacceptable is suppressed.

Civil rights - the rights a citizen has to political or social freedoms, such as the right to vote or freedom of speech.

Claim - someone's assertion of their right to something - for example, a claim to the throne.

Coalition government - a government formed by more than one political party.

Coalition, Coalitions - a temporary alliance, such as when a group of countries fights together.

Coexistence - living or existing together at the same time or in the same place.

Collective security - a policy adopted by the League of Nations, with the idea members should feel safe from attack as all nations agreed to defend each other.

Colonialism - when a country seeks to bring other territories under its control, often with the aim of dominating its economy. Religion and cultural practices may also be imposed.

Communism - the belief, based on the ideas of Karl Marx, that all people should be equal in society without government, money or private property. Everything is owned by by the people, and each person receives according to need.

Communist - a believer in communism.

Conference - a formal meeting to discuss common issues of interest or concern.

Conservative - someone who dislikes change and prefers traditional values. It can also refer to a member of the Conservative Party.

Constitution - rules, laws or principles that set out how a country is governed.

Containment - meaning to keep something under control or within limits, it often refers to the American idea of stopping the spread of communism.

Conventional - in accordance with what is considered normal or generally accepted. In military terms, it refers to non-nuclear weapons.

Cooperate, Cooperation - to work together to achieve a common aim. Frequently used in relation to politics, economics or law.

Council - an advisory or administrative body set up to manage the affairs of a place or organisation. The Council of the League of Nations contained the organisation's most powerful members.

Coup - a sudden, violent and illegal overthrow of the government by a small group - for example, the chiefs of an army.

Currency - an umbrella term for any form of legal tender, but most commonly referring to money.

D

Defect - the act of defection; to leave your country or cause for another.

Demilitarised - to remove all military forces from an area and forbid them to be stationed there.

Democracy - a political system where a population votes for its government on a regular basis. The word is Greek for 'the rule of people' or 'people power'.

Democratic - relating to or supporting the principles of democracy.

Democratisation - to introduce a democratic system or principles into a country or organisation.

GLOSSARY

Deploy - to move military troops or equipment into position or a place so they are ready for action.

Deport - to expel someone from a country and, usually, return them to their homeland.

Desegregation - a policy of removing racial segregation (separation).

Deterrent - something that discourages an action or behaviour.

Dictator - a ruler with absolute power over a country, often acquired by force.

Dictatorship - a form of government where an individual or small group has total power, ruling without tolerance for other views or opposition.

Disarmament - the reduction or removal of weaponry.

Dispute - a disagreement or argument; often used to describe conflict between different countries.

Dissent, Dissenting - to hold or express views against an idea or policy, often in politics.

Dissolution, Dissolve - the formal ending of a partnership, organisation or official body.

Doctrine - a stated principle of government policy; can also refer to a set of beliefs held and taught by a church, political party or other group.

Dollar imperialism - a phrase used by the Soviet Union's Foreign Minister, Molotov, in accusing the USA of using its economic strength to take over Europe through the Marshall Plan.

Détente - the easing of tension, especially between two countries.

E

Economic - relating to the economy; also used when justifying something in terms of profitability.

Economy - a country, state or region's position in terms of production and consumption of goods and services, and the supply of money.

Embassy - historically, a deputation sent by one ruler, state or country to another. More recently, it is also the accepted name for the official residence or offices of an ambassador.

Empire - a group of states or countries ruled over and controlled by a single monarch.

Exile - to be banned from one's original country, usually as a punishment or for political reasons.

Export - to transport goods for sale to another country.

F

Fascist - one who believes in fascism.

Federal - in US politics this means 'national', referring to the whole country rather than any individual state.

Foreign policy - a government's strategy for dealing with other nations.

Free elections - elections in which voters are free to vote without interference.

Front - in war, the area where fighting is taking place.

H

Hard line - strict and uncompromising.

I

Ideology - a set of ideas and ideals, particularly around political ideas or economic policy, often shared by a group of people.

Import - to bring goods or services into a different country to sell.

Independence, Independent - to be free of control, often meaning by another country, allowing the people of a nation the ability to govern themselves.

Industrial - related to industry, manufacturing and/or production.

Intercontinental ballistic missile - a guided ballistic missile with a minimum range of 5,500km or 3,400 miles.

Iron Curtain - a phrase used by Winston Churchill to describe the non-physical divide created by Stalin between Eastern Europe and the West.

L

Liberal - politically, someone who believes in allowing personal freedom without too much control by the government or state.

M

Merchant ships - unarmed ships used for carrying supplies and goods.

Military force - the use of armed forces.

Minister - a senior member of government, usually responsible for a particular area such as education or finance.

Monarchy - a form of government in which the head of state is a monarch, a king or queen.

Mujahideen - Islamic guerrilla fighters.

P

Poverty - the state of being extremely poor.

Predecessor - the person who came before; the previous person to fill a role or position.

President - the elected head of state of a republic.

Prevent, Preventative, Preventive - steps taken to stop something from happening.

Propaganda - biased information aimed at persuading people to think a certain way.

Prosecute - to institute or conduct legal proceedings against a person or organisation.

GLOSSARY

Proxy war - a conflict between two sides acting on behalf of other parties who are not directly involved, but who have usually supplied equipment, arms and/or money.

Purged, Purging - abrupt and often violent removal of a group of people from a place or organisation; medically, to make someone sick or induce diarrhoea as a treatment to rid them of illness.

Q

Quarantine - a period of isolation where a person or animal who has or may have a communicable disease is kept away from others.

R

Ratification, Ratified - to give formal agreement or consent to something.

Rationing - limiting goods that are in high demand and short supply.

Rebellion - armed resistance against a government or leader, or resistance to other authority or control.

Rebels - people who rise in opposition or armed resistance against an established government or leader.

Reform, Reforming - change, usually in order to improve an institution or practice.

Refugee, Refugees - a person who has been forced to leave where they live due to war, disaster or persecution.

Reparations - payments made by the defeated countries in a war to the victors to help pay for the cost of and damage from the fighting.

Repressive - a harsh or authoritarian action; usually used to describe governmental abuse of power.

Republic - a state or country run by elected representatives and an elected/nominated president. There is no monarch.

Revolution - the forced overthrow of a government or social system by its own people.

Rig, Rigged - politically, to interfere in or fix an election to determine the winner.

Riots - violent disturbances involving a crowd of people.

S

Sanctions - actions taken against states who break international laws, such as a refusal to trade with them or supply necessary commodities.

Satellite state - a country under the control of another, such as countries under USSR control during the Cold War.

Sino - is a a reference to China or something relating to China. It is a prefix which is used instead of China.

Socialism - a political and economic system where most resources, such as factories and businesses, are owned by the state or workers with the aim of achieving greater equality between rich and poor.

Soviet - an elected workers' council at local, regional or national level in the former Soviet Union. It can also be a reference to the Soviet Union or the USSR.

Sphere of influence - an area or country under the influence of another country.

Standard of living - level of wealth and goods available to an individual or group.

State of emergency - where a national emergency, disaster or crisis has occurred in which normal government procedures are suspended so it can deal with the situation.

State, States - an area of land or a territory ruled by one government.

Strike - a refusal by employees to work as a form of protest, usually to bring about change in their working conditions. It puts pressure on their employer, who cannot run the business without workers.

Summit - a formal meeting between two or more heads of government.

T

Tactic - a strategy or method of achieving a goal.

Territories, Territory - an area of land under the control of a ruler/country.

Thaw - the period of time where the relationship between the USSR and the USA improved.

Trade unions - organised groups of workers who cooperate to make their lives better at work. For example, they might negotiate for better pay and then organise a strike if one is refused.

Treaty - a formal agreement, signed and ratified by two or more parties.

U

Ultimatum - a final demand, with the threat of consequences if it is not met.

V

Veto - the right to reject a decision or proposal.

W

Western powers - a group term used to describe developed capitalist nations, such as Britain and the USA.

INDEX

A
Amin, Hafizullah - 74
Apollo-Soyuz mission - 58
Arms Race - 37
Attlee, Clement - 74

B
Batista, Fulgencio - 74
Bay of Pigs - 45
Berlin Airlift - 35
Berlin Blockade - 34
Berlin Crisis - 42
Berlin Wall - 43
Brezhnev Doctrine - 53
Brezhnev, Leonid - 75
Bulgaria, Satellite State - 27

C
CFE - 69
Carter Doctrine - 60
Churchill, Winston - 76
Cold War - 16
Comecon - 33
Cominform - 32
Conference of Tehran - 18
Conventional Armed Forces in Europe Treaty - 69
Cuban Missile Crisis - 46
Cuban Revolution - 44
Czechoslovakia, Satellite State - 25

D
De-Stalinisation - 39
Dubček, Alexander - 76
Détente - 54

E
Eisenhower, Dwight D - 77

F
FDR, the Second World War - 83
Fall of Gorbachev - 72
Fall of the Berlin Wall - 71

G
Geneva Summit - 65
Glasnost - 64
Gorbachev, Mikhail, policies and beliefs - 63
Grand Alliance - 17

H
Helsinki Conference - 57
Hotline - 48
Hungarian Uprising - 40
Hungary, Satellite State - 26

I
INF Treaty - 67
Intermediate-Range Nuclear Forces Treaty - 67
Iron Curtain Speech - 29

K
Kennan, George - 79
Kennedy, President - 80
Khrushchev, Nikita - 81

L
Limited Test Ban Treaty - 49
Long Telegram - 22
Loss of USSR control over Satellite States - 70
Loss of USSR control over eastern Europe - 70

M
Malta Summit - 69
Marshall Plan - 31
Marshall, George - 82
Moscow Summit - 68

N
NATO - 36
Nagy, Imre - 82
Non-Proliferation of Nuclear Weapons Treaty - 50
Novikov Telegram - 23
Novikov, Nikolai - 83
Novotny, Antonin - 83

O

INDEX

Outer Space Treaty - 49

P

Perestroika - 64
Poland, Satellite State - 24
Potsdam Conference - 21
Prague Spring - 51
President Carter doctrine - 75

R

Reagan and Gorbachev - 65
Reagan, Ronald - 61
Reykjavik Summit - 66
Romania, Satellite State - 27
Roosevelt, the Second World War - 83

S

SALT 2 - 58
SDI - 62
START - 70
Soviet Afghanistan War - 59
Soviet Satellite States - 23
Star Wars - 62
Strategic Arms Limitation Treaty 1 - 55
Strategic Arms Limitation Treaty 2 - 58
Strategic Arms Reduction Treaty - 70
Strategic Defense Initiative - 62

T

Taraki, Nur Muhammad - 84
Tehran Conference - 18
Truman Doctrine - 30
Truman, Harry - 84

W

Warsaw Pact - 37
Washington Summit - 67

Y

Yalta Conference - 19
Yugoslavia and the Cold War - 28

www.ingramcontent.com/pod-product-compliance
Lightning Source LLC
Chambersburg PA
CBHW050718090526
44588CB00014B/2328